W9-AVR-930

The Essence of Provence

THE ESSENCE
OF PROVENCE

The Story of l'Occitane

Pierre Magnan

Translated from the French by Richard Seaver

Arcade Publishing • New York

Copyright © 2001, 2012 by L'Occitane and Editions Denoel

English-language translation copyright © 2003, 2012 by Arcade Publishing

All Rights Reserved. No part of this book may be reproduced in any manner without the express written consent of the publisher, except in the case of brief excerpts in critical reviews or articles. All inquiries should be addressed to Arcade Publishing, 307 West 36th Street, 11th Floor, New York, NY 10018.

First published in France in 2001 under the title *L'Occitane: Une histoire vraie* by Editions Denoel

Arcade Publishing books may be purchased in bulk at special discounts for sales promotion, corporate gifts, fund-raising, or educational purposes. Special editions can also be created to specifications. For details, contact the Special Sales Department, Arcade Publishing, 307 West 36th Street, 11th Floor, New York, NY 10018 or arcade@skyhorsepublishing.com.

Arcade Publishing® is a registered trademark of Skyhorse Publishing, Inc.®, a Delaware corporation.

Visit our website at www.arcadepub.com.

10 9 8 7 6 5 4 3 2 1

Library of Congress Cataloging-in-Publication Data is available on file.

ISBN: 978-1-61145-495-6

Printed in China

To Laure,
to tell her about her father

The Essence of Provence

"When I was a kid, my constant companion as I went to school was the smell of honeysuckle." It is with these words that Olivier Baussan begins his story.

It was sometime during the second half of the 1950s, between the two Provençal towns of Ganagobie and Peyruis, that Olivier and his older brother Alain, their knapsacks slung over their shoulders, first experienced the fragrances of the lower Alps.

Of all perfumed plants, honeysuckle has the most elusive odor; you think you've captured it, only to find it gone. Even the wind doesn't carry it. You have to be there, next to the flower, literally stick your nose in it. When perfumers label a bottle with the word *honeysuckle*, they are making it up of whole cloth. It's a subjective aroma. Later on, the customers who bought the fragrance will take out the bottle and bury their noses in it. They'll close their eyes, and the very word *honeysuckle* will evoke the sterility of our impoverished lands.

In their minds' eye they conjure up the image of a single nanny goat tied to a stake in the midst of some sparse patch of vegetation. And if when autumn finally rolls around, they espy a honeysuckle branch, with its red, currantlike berries, it will quietly remind them that October is not far off.

But young Olivier had no idea then how special was the fragrance that assailed him. The breeze that coursed down from Ganagobie, bearing with it the odor of young pine trees planted thickly to form a veritable forest that, when the wind rose, was sibilant with murmurs, was implanting itself in the child's subconscious mind, forbidding him later on in life from ever forgetting it.

"The Durance River . . ." Olivier reminisces.

In 1956 and '57 I lived a stone's throw from the Durance. In those days they'd not yet built any dams. For my brother and me, it was a playground. The riverbed was often almost dry, and we played among the water holes, so deep and so limpid that it seemed as if there wasn't really any water there at all. Sometimes you could see in their depths the dark outline of a big fish, trapped there until the next flood. Yet the Durance could suddenly rise so quickly that all of a sudden it was a good three hundred feet across, bearing everything with it as the water rushed by, ricocheting off

the rocks. And when the floodwaters subsided, a mass of rocks as far as the eye could
see remained behind. We were struck by the
blinding light of the sun on those stones,
which were boiling hot. Still, we tried sitting
down on them, knowing they were so hot we
would jump to our feet, screaming at the top
of our young lungs.

And then there was the odor! It wasn't a
smell of water, but a mineral smell, from the
erosion of the riverbed after the water had
subsided. And with this smell there was silence, an unreal silence.

Such were the elements that affected Olivier Baussan's inner life from the moment when, only six months
old, he was transported from Paris to the lower Alps,
where he would remain, with a few exceptions, for the
rest of his life. The world that Olivier discovered thanks
to his parents' move was a place of beauty few people
are privileged to know. Longtime natives of Provence
have little good to say about it, all too often dismissing
it, deriding it sarcastically, burying it in its poverty. They
leave it behind without regret, pull up their roots and
move elsewhere. But their children, who have this blessed
corner of the world in their blood, grow up cursing their
parents for having taken them away.

Olivier was fortunate enough to have parents who
did just the contrary; though born elsewhere, they

came to live here no matter the consequences, here among the murmur of the Ganagobie pine trees.

Ganagobie is nothing but a hill like so many others, but it's a hill of mystery. This mystery oozes from under all the tumuli and ruins that litter its slopes, jealously preserved for future generations of archaeologists. From its sun–baked stones, its arid earth, arises a scent, an odor, a fragrance, emanations. Olivier's vocation would be born from these olfactory riches, but they gave no early promise of providing him with a decent living. A lad in shorts, he spent his early years climbing from one hill to another throughout the region, obviously unaware of what it would mean to him in the future; in a state of blissful ignorance he contemplated, surveying the Moines promenade (which was pristine countryside), the geography of virtually the entire lower Alps, from the Verdon Corridor to the Estrop Cirque, from the chimneys of Sainte–Tulle to the town of Digne hard by the Bléone River, and, making a sharp turn, the mountain of Lure, mistress of the north, where on winter evenings the Great Bear, also known as the Big Dipper, sleeps.

When the ineffable fragrances of this region (half sun, half sky) escape from the torrid soil in a hallucinatory vapor, you have a still that distills memory. A vocation can be born from memory, from the exasperated desire to bring back one's early dreams.

We begin with a poor farm, a couple with faith in their ideal, their youth, their strength — who believed that because they loved the earth, the earth would love them in turn. Poverty would soon grind down this nascent happiness. This couple, Olivier's parents, in this blessed land, would find themselves subjected to the irony of all those who truly love the land but are painfully aware of its tricks and traps, of how thankless the barren land can be, a land who knows only those who avoid the issue and forge blindly ahead.

This young couple, who had baptized their farm "Pra de l'Intra," soon experienced the slow erosion of their illusions, which one by one fell away: the tractor broke down; the herd of sheep fell ill; the sudden drought endured four months, five, as a result of which the crops all died or went to seed.

Olivier's father suffered an accident that made him an invalid. To confront the harsh conditions of the lower Alps without full possession of your physical faculties is to head straight for disaster. Some friends — Serge Fiorio, who despite his many talents did not hesitate for a moment to come with pick and shovel to help out his neighbor, and his brother Aldo — brought to the beleaguered family the full force of their friendship. In the eyes of the boy Olivier, Serge was huge, self-assured, a veritable rampart against adversity. Striding the land from one end to the other, Serge was the perfect incarnation of the hero of the Provençal writer Jean Giono (thanks to whose dithyrambic hymns to this patch of earth, no doubt, Oliver's parents had pulled up their Parisian roots). Giono the poet had only dreamed of his hero; in Serge, here he was in flesh and blood, a man full of reason and common sense, his feet firmly on the ground. One can presume that Serge had not read any of Giono's works, and certainly he was in no way influenced by Giono. He seized the lower Alps in his grasp and made its light the yeast of his life.

At times this black-haired painter, this giant with astrakhan curls, a stubborn brow, and the force of a battering ram, this pillar of strength, would bend down toward the child Olivier, squat in front of him, and try to make him believe they were both the same size.

"So, how is our little king doing today?" he would smile and say.

One day when Serge was on his way to lunch with the Baussans at Manosque, he spotted from above a child racing along the boulevard de la Plaine, his hair streaming in the wind. The fleeting image of that child, a wonderful apparition, remained with him throughout the morning. "Imagine my surprise," he said, "when I arrived to find myself seated next to this same child at lunch. It was Olivier."

Then, to add insult to injury — if the recalcitrant soil, land resistant to any and all efforts to dominate it, its failure to yield more than the most meager of harvests, and backbreaking work that offered little or no return were not enough — came the worst winter in a hundred years, the winter of 1956.

Until the end of January that year, the climate had been incredibly mild. Then, in a single night — the night of February 2 and 3 — everything still alive and healthy in the vegetable world, everything that, however timidly, had reason to believe that spring was not far off, exploded, was leveled, torn to shreds, wiped out. A silent breath of air came straight down from Siberia, so silent that it woke no one. In a flash it stole the Baussans' entire future. Anyone who has not seen the olive trees in February 1956 does not know the full meaning of the word *despair*. Whole orchards turned overnight into dead wood, their trunks split asunder, their bark hanging in shreds, as if some interior explosion had skinned them alive. After the devastating wind had passed, it began to snow — for a month, then two. For a happy few, the winter of 1956 was a blessing in disguise: for years some people in Provence had dreamed of a catastrophe that would rid them of their olive groves so they could plant vineyards. For the Baussans, however, it was the beginning of the end. For them the olive trees, seen from afar in Paris, had been a symbol, a goal, an image of the promised land. They had even named their second son after the blessed tree. I can see them every morning during that winter of 1956, trying to cope with the vision of their martyred symbol: the olive trees had died an instant death, their leaves turned the color of rot and fallen to the ground.

Olivier once described his father to me as an epicurean intellectual. Though I never knew him, I can nonetheless understand how devastated he was. He was the father of two young children, his wife was pregnant, and the upcoming seasons promised nothing but blood, sweat, and tears. How far removed they were now from the romantic world of the poet Giono, who had mesmerized and seduced them into pulling up their roots and completely changing their lives!

I can also picture Olivier, in that winter of 1956, trudging the accursed two miles to school. The cold and snow had killed the land's fragrance, and Provence was in mourning for its aromas and for the olive trees that had colored its slopes for a thousand years. The only survivors of that economic disaster — though not for long — were a smattering of goats who formed a huddle of heat at the far end of the stable. Goats are the sisters of charity. God knows what miserable food they need to sustain themselves and to provide milk. In February 1956, for hay the Baussans had only stalks of lavender from which the essence had been extracted, stored in a shed on the property. The goats, having nothing better to do, sidled over, sniffed the stalks, and, believe it or not — choosing to ignore the notion of despair — decided, until things took a turn for the better, to make do with this meager provender. As a result, that winter saw the Baussans graced not only with milk but with good milk, scented with lavender, which was prophetic.

Olivier used to arrive at school each morning different from all the others, thanks to the lavender-laced goat milk. And with him came his faithful dog — a huge dog that would flop down below his desk and snore away until eleven o'clock rolled around. His classmates, all natives of this harsh, unforgiving land, would nudge one another and whisper, "That's the Baussan kid. You know, the son of the Parisians. They're starving; they eat *weeds!*" Which translated: They feed themselves on the grass of the mountain slopes that even goats refuse to touch. For those who have enough to eat, not to eat one's fill is a defect, if not a sin.

To hear Olivier speak of this period, however, one does not get the impression that he suffered from this ostracism by those who thought of themselves as his betters, at least not consciously — for just because someone doesn't react doesn't mean that affronts don't sink down into the subconscious.

Nonetheless, with the help of Serge Fiorio and his brother Aldo, the Baussans did hold out for another three or four years following the winter of 1956, bound to that slave ship, enduring the terrible farm, the unforgiving land, all the elements against them, and the mocking surliness of the country people, who looked down upon those with a different accent. But bad luck can hold people in its viselike grip for just so long; the battle being unequal, the Baussans finally threw in the towel.

In all their simple good-heartedness, the local peasants not only accepted but applauded the Baussans' failure. Don't think for a minute our people are charitable: bad luck frightens them as if it were an epidemic. Those who fail leave behind them a kind of negative file, like a police record.

"There goes Baussan, one more smart fellow who thought he could feed off the land without paying his dues."

Not a trace of pity! "So, you wanted to return to the land, eh? See what you got!"

From that moment on, doubtless somewhere deep in his subconscious, in his eight-year-old child's brain, Olivier must have planned out, however dimly, how to get revenge for his family's humiliation.

For the moment, however, the Baussans were really up against it. Picture this, if you will: a father who is handicapped; two youngsters, and a third on the way; a family thrown out of their house onto the street.

Olivier's big dog followed him around as if nothing had happened. He followed him to a two-room shack, where the destitute family at last found a sort of refuge: no running water, no electricity, no heat, no facilities, but at least a roof over their heads. Olivier remembers all too well his father setting forth each morning, shovel in hand, to dig latrines for the entire family as far as possible from the shack.

This situation lasted for three long years, years during which Olivier's baby sister came into this world of deprivation. Oh, let's not paint too dark a picture: it was not yet Christ in the stable, but we're only a step or two away. Meanwhile, those who witnessed the fall of the house of Baussan looked on in sardonic silence.

This brings us to 1960. At the end of that painful period, M. Baussan finally landed a job writing for the local Manosque newspaper, the *Méridional,* or *Voice of the South.* The provincial press was flourishing at this time. Prominent not only locally but even nationally, the *Méridional* was a conservative paper — Provence *is* conservative — that went to great lengths to please local political power broker Gaston Defferre, himself the owner of another newspaper, the *Provençal.* Defferre, mayor of Marseille in the 1980s, was also president of the regional council of Paca, thus a personage to be reckoned with. All of which goes a long way toward explaining how the *Méridional* could offer its local correspondents a living wage.

So the Baussans left their run-down shack and moved into a housing project on the outskirts of Manosque. For Olivier, this meant not only leaving behind the countryside — however primitive — but moving into a soulless warren, where people of all sorts were jammed in together without any semblance of fraternal relations or common bond. This was a terrible shock to the boy, the first disillusionment of his young life. The shack next to the railroad tracks may have had no amenities, but it was still in the country, still set in the context of nature. But this housing project, with no light and little air — anyone who knew these 1960s Manosque projects will know what I mean — seemed to be built to punish people, not house them.

To add insult to injury, Olivier's dog could not come along. True, at the cabin he had been forbidden to come in, but he could still sleep outside or, during the day, find refuge with one member of the family or another. The rest of the time he would wander off on some canine adventure in the nearby woods. There was no such freedom to wander in Manosque; he would frighten the neighbors. No dog, no soothing breeze, nor any longer the reassuring odor of lavender or honeysuckle. "This abrupt contact with civilization, this feeling of being deprived of my freedom for the first time, was terribly painful to me," Olivier remembers.

In fact, all of his youthful memories of Manosque are painful, apparently. In school he was a mediocre student. He made little or no effort to fit in, to join the others, with whom he felt he had little in common. He did make some friends, however, and one day, when he and several other pals went swimming in a nearby canal used to irrigate the crops, he nearly drowned. He was fished out by one of the other boys as he went down for the third time. No question, Olivier and Manosque were not made for each other. He would return to that town only when he could deal with it as an equal.

Meanwhile, his father was transferred to Digne, a larger town, as bureau chief of the *Méridional* there, inching the family fortunes up another notch. What was more, Digne, though still a city, was, unlike Manosque, a place full of poetry. The Bléone River ran past, mountains rose all around, and in contrast to Manosque's constant noise, Digne was a quiet town. At night all was silent, which suited a shy and retiring child — far from an outgoing, rough-and-ready type — who didn't even play soccer.

In Digne, Olivier discovered the second important influence on his young life, Serge Fiorio being the first. When he met Alexandra David-Néel she was pushing eighty. Haughty and cold as ice, she frightened the local youngsters, but she also fascinated them. For one thing, she had traveled the world, visiting all sorts of exotic places, and that notion of travel grafted itself onto the wandering imagination of the boy Olivier.

Alexandra's fame was limited, for this was a time when the media, nowadays insatiable in its efforts to seek out and exploit exotic personages, was less prominent and pervasive. With several of his classmates, Olivier paid her a visit. "She scared the bejesus out of me," Olivier recalls, "especially her legs, which were all swollen and blue. And her eyes also frightened me."

But Alexandra had seen Tibet, and though her body may have been back in Digne, her heart and soul still wandered on the roof of the world, in that strange country where it never rains, this land where everyone goes about on foot, their eyes fixed on the distant horizon as they stride along, to what purpose and toward what goal she couldn't say. "And the Brahmaputre?" she asked the boys. "Can you imagine that enormous body of water, which crisscrosses the entire expanse of this country where it never rains? Is it any wonder that the people who live there seem strange, that they run rather than walk? Running after what? Their ideas?

Probably trying to figure out the jokes that Nature has played on them."

Olivier sat at the feet of this enormous, formless woman, who bore that fabulous country within her, was permeated with it to the very marrow of her bones, her essence. Just as she and that country were one, the huge gap between the woman and the boy simply disappeared.

She spoke of motionless flowers, covered with sand, that never bloom, awaiting a spring that never comes to incite them to open. These enormous flowers remain buds, and yet when you cut them open, down the middle, you can see that they are fully equipped with stamens and pistils, everything necessary to reproduce, bring forth a new generation of flowers. How do you explain that? Or how does Nature?

When Olivier left that house, where everything was so strange, where talk summoned up far-off places, he found himself back in Digne, listening to the soothing sound of the flowing waters of the Bléone River. He and his schoolmates went and stood on the old bridge, which would later disappear, swept away in a sudden flood. The Bléone is not the Brahmaputre, to be sure, but if the snow-covered flanks of the lower Alps suddenly turn black for weeks on end, the melting snow can turn this peaceful trickle of water into a roaring torrent, a real river, scraping its bed clean of rocks. These giant stones, together with the corpses of trees the floodwaters have felled along the way, hurl themselves against the bridge — any bridge — and destroy it as if it had been struck by a grenade.

But that evening, all those autumn evenings, everything was peaceful, silent, and calm. For those who don't know how to appreciate the special quality of this discreet city, which comes only upon long knowledge and reflection, Digne can seem the dullest place on Earth. And in a man's life, youth is the period most prone to boredom, for it's a time of waiting. Dreaming and waiting.

"Someday I'll do this, someday I'll . . ." Olivier must have said to himself countless times as he leaned on the balustrade of the bridge over the Bléone, searching, stubbornly searching, until the roadway of the bridge itself was swept away in the flood.

A prisoner in Digne? That's the impression one gets from Olivier's endless contemplations, his seasons of boredom on the banks of the Bléone. But in fact Olivier was the prisoner of his youth. He was aching to compress time, to move ahead as quickly as he feasibly could.

Fortunately, there was the world of books. Olivier's father had always been an avid reader, a virtue he passed on to his son. The first book to capture his attention at age fifteen was *War and Peace*. Tolstoy's world was as far removed in time and space as David–Néel's Tibet, just as unusual, strange, and distressing, yet somehow tangible. Digne, plus Tolstoy, plus events beginning to gather on the horizon that would soon strike down, as if by lightning, the old values, or at least those that would not be missed by the partisans of the new world order, some of whose doctrines would be channeled toward new philosophies meant to incite the masses once again: such was the climate of Olivier's youth.

In May 1968 Olivier Baussan turned sixteen. Since his family's economic situation, though improved, was still only slightly above the poverty level, Olivier had no expectations from that quarter. He got up at four in the morning to deliver the local paper to its subscribers in Digne and the suburbs on his motor scooter. After making his rounds, he headed off to school, where he was a mediocre student — good at writing and French, much less so at other subjects. He was a bit of a loner, holding himself aloof from his schoolmates' greediness, their coarse materialism. They guzzled their way through life without examining it, he felt, without analyzing or savoring it. Olivier, on the contrary, felt it sliding past him, silky, full, confident. And life was whispering to him this divine truth: "Believe in only what you can grasp and personally understand about me. And don't believe anything others say about me."

Olivier carried a volume of Rimbaud in his pocket, having fallen in love with this nineteenth-century poet, this literary outlaw who believed only in himself and his own values. "In literature, poetry was by far my favorite," he says. "When I was still in my teens, I hit the road with Rimbaud in my pocket, alone. I hitchhiked throughout Europe. I went up as far as Sweden, Holland, and Denmark. Not a penny to my name. I slept like a homeless person. In Copenhagen, I slept in a storefront window."

He could just as easily have slept in that revolting train station, among the baggage lockers, among the bird droppings and the vomit of those who shoot up with whatever drug is available in an attempt to find themselves, to discover the genius that always seems just beyond their reach. He met self-proclaimed prophets who thrashed about, their arms outstretched, to gather unto them ten or twenty disciples committed to their woolly-minded cosmogony.

But Olivier still had Rimbaud close to his heart.

Adrift himself, he lent a helping hand to the druggies he found along the way. They resented him for not joining them in their magic world of drugs, for turning his back on the infinite wonders they dangled before him; like them he was poor but different, refusing to take the ultimate step.

"What always saved me," he says, "what kept me from taking that fatal step into the world of drugs, was poetry. Because I saw drugs everywhere I looked, I saw the addicts themselves, and that's what saved me, not only having poetry in my pocket but knowing in my heart and mind that there was another ideal, another goal, even if I wasn't sure exactly what it was."

I picture him raising his slim volume of Rimbaud, the way others raise a crucifix, to stand between himself and temptation. Words, magic words that give power, even if you don't even try to understand them.

A teary tincture washes
Over cabbage–green skies:
Beneath the tender young tree
Seeping onto slickers

Very special moonlight rays
With ripening spheres,
Knock your knobby knees together
My darling ugly ducklings.

How we loved each other way back then
My ugly blue–eyed one.
Those were times of soft–boiled eggs
And chickweed as well.

And so Olivier returned to Digne unharmed, to discover the effects of May 1968. His schoolmates were in a state of flux and fury. Freedom was the byword: We must seize our freedom! A bit difficult in a city where freedom has always existed, and been taken for granted, as long as anyone can remember. No matter: you have to *proclaim* that you're free. How do you do that? Vandalize the lycée, that's how, and the sooner the better! A long weekend was coming up, an excellent time to lock the door to the chemistry class, plug up the washbasin drains, and turn on the spigots full blast. Olivier might have been a degree less stupid than the others, but he had no desire to stand out. In this area, intelligence was often seen as synonymous with betrayal: he who possessed it had best make himself as inconspicuous as possible. Olivier didn't betray his colleagues. Thus he was the first, probably the only, culprit to get caught on Tuesday morning. Dragged before the disciplinary committee of the school, he was expelled.

Olivier would finish his high school studies on his own, by correspondence. He passed his baccalaureate in Aix-en-Provence and immediately enrolled in the department of modern literature at the University of Aix.

His interests and leanings were still toward nature. Even the least important cities, he felt, reduced him to a state of slavery. In a world moving toward technology, to enroll in the classics was already a declaration of nonconformism. For a brief moment at Digne, Olivier had flirted with the far left youth movement, but without the kind of conviction that breeds real militants; he did it more to please his classmates than anything else.

"At Aix," Olivier recalls thirty years later, "politics was very much the order of the day, especially pro-Maoist — this was, you remember, the time of the 'great leap forward' — but I was much more interested in the problems of racism and anti-Semitism, anything that implied the denigration of a human being simply because of his race or religion. I was far more ready to march in the streets for that cause than for Mao or Ho Chi Minh." But what bothered young Olivier most was not knowing whether he or his college classmates were right, whether or not he should conform to the peremptory affirmations of his friends: "If you're not with us, you're against us." That threat brought more people to the political table than did real conviction.

Olivier found himself caught between the proverbial rock and a hard place: poor as a church mouse, he wanted to live in the countryside, and he dreaded the idea that he was not doing the right thing, that he was heading in the wrong direction. "It's a question of finding one's roots," he notes. "Once I found mine, I defended them tooth and nail. But the fact is, it took me a long time to find them."

It took me a long time to find them. In his several years at the university he undertook Lacanian psychoanalysis, which not only cost him a pretty penny but went on for years. It's difficult to feel obliged to enter psychoanalysis because you're unsure of yourself, because you feel that others may be right and you, wrong; because you feel you're somehow not made in the same mold as everyone else, and that if you were, you'd be happy and well-balanced. The fact is, Olivier was fine as he was, but the world into which he'd been thrust was all topsy-turvy. *He* was not out of step: the world around him was.

As for his constant state of near-poverty, no one ever offered to lend him a helping hand. When the school day was over, his well-to-do classmates went home to Mama and Papa without giving a thought to how he might be spending his evening in his garret. Garrets are for poets, and they alone know how to endure them.

It's difficult to record Olivier's life between his seventeenth and twenty-second year. While he was a student at Aix, he met Anne Marius Martine, a fellow student, and before you knew it, they had a child, Laurent. "Can you believe it!" Olivier says to me. "There I was, barely twenty, and already a father!"

To keep body and soul together for all three, Olivier took a job as a supervisor at the Manosque lycée while he was still a full-time student at the University of Aix, thirty miles away. "I also waited on tables at the famous Aix café, Aux Deux Garçons. Even that wasn't enough, so in the predawn hours I began delivering newspapers, as I had at Digne years before. Then I took a job as a traveling salesman peddling jewelry, lured into it by a man who promised that it was a sure way to get rich quick, the only rub being that I was never paid, or only when I managed to worm something out of him."

And yet at this same time fate was waving a sign in front of Olivier's nose, though he would not immediately respond. Together with a friend, he had the idea of manufacturing women's handbags out of linen and printing various advertisements on them, like handbags they had seen from Greece. So off he went to a store in Aix called Carneby. "Carneby was a women's clothing store, slightly exotic. I went to see the proprietor as if I were a traveling salesman. The only problem was, I wasn't a company. I didn't exist. It was a bit difficult telling the guy, 'Sorry, I can't give you an invoice,' but he nonetheless placed an order, and we managed to manufacture the handbags. I already had a certain sense of commerce, and had figured out the basics: someone places an order, you deliver the merchandise and specify the terms, which are honored; that's the basis of the entire affair." With his modest handbags, Olivier took his first tentative steps in the world of commerce: honoring his commitment.

In his next, equally tentative step, he went door-to-door as an insurance salesman, spouting the same spiel time after time, without success. Despite his best efforts, he never sold a single policy. The underwriters, taking pity on the young man and recognizing his valiant efforts, rewarded him by paying the insurance on his tin lizzie, the legendary 2CV, that funny-looking Citroën concoction built after World War II to offer France's car-hungry population an automobile at a reasonable price.

Still, since both Olivier and his wife were pulling down regular salaries, however modest, they managed to put aside a bit of savings. This was essential, because Olivier's psychoanalysis was costing more and more as time went on. Olivier meanwhile blindly pursued his studies in modern literature, not really knowing why or where it was leading. He had no intention of becoming a professor, of ending up in academe. He was counting on the analysis to help him find his way, to be the forceps that would pull him into the world of his chosen profession. At this point he couldn't envisage what this might be, much less plan for it. Nonetheless, he sensed that it was embedded within him, secret and mysterious, to such a degree that he would need to overcome all sorts of obstacles to drag it into the light of day. But he was somehow convinced that some day in the not too distant future, it would be revealed. In all fairness, how in the world could this young man ever imagine — coming as he did from a family of idealists whose own dream was to return to the land, live off the land — that he was born for the world of commerce?

But he was still a long way from fulfilling that underlying promise. A number of failures lay ahead. First, the farm at Reillanne, with the promising name: *Vallon des Oiseaux* — Vale of the Birds. This was an era when many people were turning their backs on the "normal" world, the so-called rat race, and fleeing to the countryside, where life was presumably simpler and the air fresh and pure, rejoining reality only when their stomachs rumbled with hunger. History would label them "hippies," and Olivier counted more than a few among his friends. Since he alone had a regular income, however meager, he was their main if not sole source of support. But his income was not nearly enough to feed this errant band, and so, taking after his father, he had the idea of farming the land: a few goats, a vegetable garden, some hens and rabbits. It was Serge Fiorio who

found the Vale of the Birds. But the poetic name dis-
guised a harsh, unyielding earth.

Olivier's salary sufficed to pay the farm's monthly
rent, at least. "To all intents and purposes, I was subsi-
dizing them," Olivier remembers,

> because we lived off my salary, and whatever
> we managed to glean from the land was not
> enough to feed us. For the most part, they
> were people just passing through. I began
> with a few rabbits and chickens. One morning
> I woke up to find them all dead of myxo-
> matosis. Still, to make contact with the land
> again, to breathe the country air, was very im-
> portant to me. I went out and set traps. We
> lived off the small game that I caught every
> day. We also caught crayfish, which I carried
> in the same little buckets I used to play with
> on the beach when I was a kid. I was living in
> the woods. It's there that I rediscovered that
> strength — I can see just in describing it to you
> how emotional I get — my great moments of
> strength, which I always rediscover whenever
> I'm in contact with Nature. I would leave the
> farm early in the morning, check my traps,
> carve up the game I'd snared, go back, and
> prepare lunch. I'd first discovered the primi-
> tive unspoiled life in reading Thoreau's *Walden
> Pond* when I was young. He was for me one of

the world's first ecologists. And it was that natural life he described that I aspired to.

Still, he was swimming upstream in the world he had chosen, for all his hippie friends were trying to convince him that theirs was the one way, the only possible road to salvation. While all Olivier wanted was to live a simple life, everyone around him was trying to convince him that he should ascend to higher levels, political and personal.

"That life at Aix, that politicized life, that life of so-called intellectuals, wasn't for me. All I wanted was the simple life. Even if for a long time I pretended to be an intellectual, even if I could discuss Kierkegaard and Barthes with the best of them, that wasn't my thing. I loved Lacan, because everyone else did. But the problem was, I soon found that virtually everyone was simply spewing forth, in their own words, exactly what their professors had laid on them the day or week before. I suppose I entered psychoanalysis more out of principle than conviction."

That may be true, but meanwhile Olivier's life had become sheer hell. He was juggling the roles of a dormitory adviser, a university student, a father, and a husband to a woman with whom he rarely made love anymore, with whom he finally broke up. He engaged in sexual escapades with one woman after another, with no more real conviction than he had for Lacan or Kierkegaard, and, to be honest, in a true romance with an English professor whose name, twenty-five years later, he nevertheless has trouble remembering. Our young man was thrashing wildly about, given to various promiscuities, both intellectual and sexual, while chastising the unruly beasts under his tutelage at the lycée. Pretty much a lost soul, our Olivier, at this point in his life.

And then, one serendipitous day, one of those characters impossible to describe — tall, dark, and bathed in his own self-importance — entered Olivier Baussan's life. One evening, in the town of Manosque in the eastern part of Provence, Olivier met a certain André Botte, who was holding court in a local café, talking about ecology. This was the first time that Olivier, at that point a student of modern literature at the University of Aix and a dormitory adviser at the lycée of Apt, had ever heard the term, but what the man was saying seemed so obvious to him that he couldn't refrain from smiling.

"What are you laughing at? Yes, you over there," said the odd duck of a man, who was used to being taken seriously.

"Because I was listening to what you were saying, and I thought it made sense."

To which the man thundered, "So tell me now, what do you wash your hair with?"

"With Marseille soap," Olivier responded.

"Which automatically makes you an ecologist," the Man of the Moment concluded. He pointed a peremptory finger in Olivier's direction, as if he were anointing him. The counter of the bar was being turned into a baptistery.

"So," Olivier went on,

I suddenly found myself involved in a thing called the Green Life. Botte was in the process of setting up some sort of woolly-minded, nebulous organization in the framework of utopian ecology. He was gathering subscriptions for a kind of cooperative by promising that he was going to manufacture various ecologically pure bath oils and essences. In his earlier days he had promoted a number of products. In fact, my father, who was writing for the local paper *Le Méridional*, had devoted an article to him. My parents had several samples of his products, which they had never opened, because the bottles were so beautiful. Before you could blink an eye, Botte had appointed me as his secretary — without salary of course, since he didn't have a penny to his name. For the next six months I witnessed how he did his thing. I was a pretty good writer, words flowed easily from my pen, and I used to write his speeches, what he was planning to say to any given audience, for it turned out he couldn't write; he was completely illiterate.

This kind of character had always been familiar in Provence; hailing from God knows where, in various shapes and forms, large or small, fat or thin, but always with deep, booming voices, always peremptory, addressing themselves not to any single individual, not even to a crowd but *ex cathedra urbi et orbi*, like the pope himself, their heads held self-assuredly high as they gazed not at but over the heads of their audience, ignoring at the same time as appealing to them.

The locals, it should be noted, who were in other circumstances fiercely distrustful, were oddly fond of these shady tightrope artists, who, while not openly calling them country bumpkins, made them feel as much at every possible moment. As a result the subscriptions to Botte's ecological enterprise poured in.

"He was a little rough around the edges," Olivier remembers,

> a bit of a boor. At the point I met him, he was probably in his mid–fifties, and he had the ability to wrap you around his little finger. People were lining up with their checks in hand to join the Green Life. It was a cooperative, he stressed, which meant that when you joined, you owned part of the organization. And he promised one and all, each would soon be receiving various ecologically pure offerings: bubble baths, soaps, shampoos, what-

ever. . . . I didn't go to many of his meetings, because I was still a student, and also trying to rebuild this broken-down old farm I had bought for a song and was trying to make habitable. But I did go often enough to remain intrigued and interested. André summoned people to attend his meetings, and they came. "If you call them, they will come" seemed to be his motto. Even a number of bankers from one of the country's major financial institutions attended. One day, he literally took my breath away. He went to the Renault automobile dealer in Manosque and ordered not one but two cars. And as I said, the man didn't have a penny to his name! He introduced me as his secretary. While awaiting delivery of his two brand-new cars, he asked for a loaner car, which they gave him on the spot. When he failed to return it, the dealer had to send the bailiffs out to repossess it!

Botte was, among other things, the sworn enemy of Robert Morel and his wife, for whom I had the highest admiration. They had founded a small publishing house dedicated to making beautiful, limited-edition books that, however handsome, had little or no chance of penetrating the commercial market. For André Botte, the past master of packaging, this was a sheer waste of time and talent. I kept telling myself, "I'm dealing with a pure nutcase!" but I was nonetheless staggered by the man, fascinated to see this mad hatter seduce whole masses of people, who succumbed to his charm like so many flies to flypaper. He was capable of making up his life as he went along. Every morning he woke up with a thousand ideas in his head, none of which would ever see the light of day. He'd call upon artisans, publicists, graphic designers, and order 50,000 labels for nonexistent products. They — the artists and artisans — would think they'd finally landed the big fish. And he'd invite them. To the local bar, any bar in sight. Everywhere he went, he was greeted with open arms. And as he left, he would wave back from the door: "You can put all that on my tab!" He'd shout that out, in front of everyone, in that stentorian voice that brooked no contradiction. It was pure, unadulterated charisma, with a lot of hot air thrown in.

This special gift, the result of divine grace, was displayed with such consummate artistry in Olivier's presence that he too was totally seduced. He may have been conquered, but he was nonetheless appalled, for Olivier was a profoundly honest man. It bothered him more and more to be constantly involved with a downright crook. "Listen, André," he told Botte, "all these bubble baths and essences of this and that, why don't you actually manufacture them? I'm ready and willing to go out and peddle them for you."

And André, whose life strategy was never to do a lick of work, to live on the gullibility of the public, responded by insulting Olivier, saying that if he was so keen on *making* something, then he damn well better plan on doing it on his own.

"It must be said that he was tipsy every day," Olivier admitted.

> His lady friend, Madeleine Chardonnel, who was also his decorator, helped me a lot. Between us we conspired to entice him into really manufacturing some products to go with his endless spiels. He told us there was nothing to it, all you had to do was buy some Texapont N40, which you could buy at such and such a place — he knew that for sure because he had done it fifteen years earlier. Texapont, I later learned, was a vegetable-based ingredient, containing copra oil, that created the foam. As he talked, I noted down in my head what he said: "Texapont N40, into which you mix the essential oils, and before you knew it you have your bubble bath, as

simple as pie. No need for any highfalutin chemists." But the fact of my having challenged him to actually manufacture something irritated the hell out of old André. "You're on your own!" he grumbled. "Just don't expect any help from me!"

"All right," I said, "That's fine with me."

But he, who was nobody's fool (I've learned a lot from this guy), called me the next day on the telephone: "I've thought it over," he said, "and with all I've told you, all the trade secrets I've revealed, I want you to sign some papers! You owe me 50,000 francs. I'll give you my trademark, 'The Heights of Provence,' and you can promote and sell my bubble bath to your heart's content. Guaranteed to slim you down and pick you up. All that's worth at least 50,000 francs. You can pay me whenever you have the money."

He came over, spread some papers out in front of me, and got me to sign them, acknowledging I owed him 50,000 francs! Since I was now in debt to him, I now had no choice but to start producing these wonderful bubble baths!

A second serendipitous encounter: as he was wandering though the countryside one day, Olivier discovered a rusted old still with iron wheels, on the side of a dirt road running through a lavender field. Lying on its side, its smokestack pointing skyward, it probably hadn't been used for twenty years. He bought it for the price of its copper. But it's one thing to own a still, quite another to make it work. Not to mention transporting it from its lopsided location in the lavender field and giving it a roof over its head. The acquisition might have been Olivier's response to André Botte's challenge, or because he desperately needed that money; but it all happened just when young Olivier was breaking up with Jane, an English girl who'd been teaching in southern France and was now on her way back to England.

It was a love story such as one rarely encounters, for though the object of Olivier's desire was no longer there, gone forever, for him love lingered on. Thus, in the throes of a bad case of unrequited love, Olivier nonetheless managed to distill his first essence of rosemary.

The welcoming hills and valleys of Provence are filled with this aromatic plant, which the locals have never figured out how to put to good use, except perhaps to wrap around a saddle of a rabbit before roasting it. So here we have these arid thickets of rosemary, with their tiny, delicately purple flowers, this prickly rosemary whose scent is neither an aroma nor a flavor. Love had done its job; Jane had gone back home, never to be seen again. Alone and adrift, this student, he of the white, unsullied hands, overnight became a peasant, a worker. To distill is no big deal, but for a solitary man, picking rosemary is a truly arduous task. This wonderful herb has to be cut; though it's not really thorny, it's still tough and prickly on the hands. To make things easier, Olivier transported the still to the site where the rosemary grew.

So it is that in the course of 1976–77, a strange-looking equipage wobbled along through the countryside: a rickety, much-abused still with its loose rivets clanging in the wind, hooked up more or less securely to an ancient 2CV that Olivier had patched up with his own hands (over the course of the years, he fixed up as many as twelve old 2CVs, buying them moribund and putting them back on the road).

First destination: the Laye, a stream that flows beneath the village of Limans. This little stream, with its crystalline voice, would supply the water; the slope of the hillside leading up to Longo Maï would furnish the rosemary; and the dead undergrowth and abandoned building material along the almost dry streambed would furnish the firewood. All the elements were in place, and one morning the air filled with a fragrant odor that at first hesitated to sublimate itself, was no more than an element of the still air. Who knows? Perhaps it wove itself into the passing wind to reach the shores of England, an elegiac, nostalgic message to a lost love.

As he stared into the glowing embers heating the rundown still, what could Olivier have been thinking that day? Of a dream still undefined? Was he still carrying the volume of Rimbaud in his pocket? Was he even dimly aware that he was in the process of making his own poetry, a solid poetry? Of discovering at long last what he was born to be and to do?

To undertake this new, unaccustomed work, Olivier outfitted himself in a jacket and trousers of country corduroy and a pair of clodhoppers. But he soon realized that if he was going to tame Mother Nature, he would have to get rid of his new outfit and trade it for something simpler.

I asked Olivier several times if he could remember the thoughts that went through his mind as the first drops of distilled rosemary dripped into the waiting receptacle below. But that initial harvest of exotic fragrance was so interwoven with the extraordinary explosion of events that would soon follow, it was impossible for memory to separate them.

Let us imagine for a moment, then, this twenty-three-year-old student, father of a two-year-old son, his family already under stress, changing his clothes at night to wait on tables at a café to put a bit more bread on the table, still pursuing his studies in modern literature without really believing in them. To make matters worse, he has just signed some legal documents putting him into debt to a crook, to the tune of 50,000 francs.

As under stress as he was, Olivier somehow managed to find an old shed, which he rented for the proverbial song. Here he brought his still, now cleaned and ready to serve. The shed contained a solid stone sink, and in this Olivier produced his first bubble baths, in bottles graced with labels scraped up from God knows where — from his students, perhaps. Olivier himself drove his first meager harvest to the nearby towns — Manosque, Forcalquier, Digne — where he peddled it to the local merchants. One can picture their initial pained expressions, their doubtful looks, as they took the bottles to the back of the shop, there to examine and mull, then to return and say that, sorry, it didn't fit their line. But miracle of miracles, one person said yes, then another. By noon he had sold most of his stock, which was the good news. The bad news was that he would have to return the next day to his shed and fire up the old still again.

One thing Olivier learned that day was that his labels just would not do. However good the product, the labels could not be taken seriously. In the village of Tourettes, near Forcalquier, someone told him, there was a graphic arts studio. He drove over, introduced himself to the owner, Yves Perrousseaux, and said: "I won't beat around the bush, monsieur. I haven't got a penny to my name. I want to sell aromatic products that I produce myself. I need some labels. Can you make them for me? On credit?"

Perrousseaux could hardly believe his ears. He called over a colleague. Both of them looked at this young man, who hadn't a penny and wasn't afraid to say so, over, from head to foot.

"Of course we will," they said in unison, without having consulted each other.

"But," says Yves, "with a trade name like 'The Heights of Provence,' you'll never get anywhere. Doomed to failure."

And it was there, driving down out of Tourettes, as he passed the hamlet of Escuyers, that Olivier was struck by that strange and mysterious voice that we poets know so well, though we can never explain where it comes from, that interior voice that makes itself heard when all seems lost.

"You'll call it l'Occitane!" said the voice.

It was perfect: the ancient language of Provence, fraught with all sorts of cultural overtones, l'Occitane encompassed not only a region but a whole cultural identity. The timing was also propitious: local regions were hoisting their proud banners, reviving their almost lost languages, demanding from the central government the right to give their streets and squares Provençal names. The mayor of the little village of Buoux refused to speak anything except l'Occitane-Provençal, citing the example of Pablo Neruda.

"So I'll call my company l'Occitane!" Olivier repeated to himself over and over.

Armed with that brand-new name, Olivier stopped off at Forcalquier. On the boulevard Latourette was a sleepy little hardware store, run by a certain Mme. Clément. To survive she sold all sorts of goods in addition to the standard fare, for she had been struggling desperately ever since two supermarkets appeared on the scene, one on each side of town.

Olivier transformed himself from a neophyte manufacturer of herbal essences into a fast-talking salesman (something he had picked up from Botte), but all Mme. Clément saw was a nice young man, clearly penniless, with his sad little bottle of merchandise that he placed on the counter. She was moved to place an order.

"Three hundred and fifty francs' worth," Olivier noted. "That was the amount of my initial order. In 1970s dollars, that came to about seventy cents."

"But you can't buy this," Olivier told her, "it's only a sample."

"Don't worry about it," Mme. Clément assured him, she who had a heart of gold; "you'll bring me the real material when you have it."

As Olivier told his analyst that evening, he thought he had died and gone to heaven. The rest of the day he spent making the rounds of all the nearby towns — Aix, Volx, Manosque, Sainte-Tulle, Corbières, Peyrolles, Meyragues — the same miserable little sample in his hand. In the course of making these rounds, he was struck by another idea: it was all well and good to manufacture these products, but shouldn't he have some legal protection? Some kind of real company?

"My idea was to form some kind of workers' cooperative," Olivier said, "which was very much in vogue back then. That's what the big watch company LIP had done, so that was good enough for me. Then one day I ran into an accountant I knew and respected, Hélène Aguillon, and when she heard what I'd done, she threw up her hands and cried, 'That's a terrible idea! The commercial courts take a very dim view of those cooperatives. You must absolutely get yourself properly incorporated.' The only problem was, to form a cooperative cost nothing; to incorporate cost twenty thousand francs. Twenty thousand francs I didn't have."

So Olivier canvassed the family to raise the needed money. His uncle came through with 5,000 francs, and — miracle of miracles — his ex-mother-in-law put up the rest (remember, Olivier and his wife were long estranged).

So here was Olivier with a properly incorporated company, a trickle of orders, a still, and the feeling that there was a pot of gold somewhere at the end of the rainbow.

But that isn't all. This isn't a fairy tale. I'm talking about the power of intuition among people who are truly intelligent, about the power of the human fraternity when it decides to join forces and pull together, when it has decided to affect someone's destiny. Anyway, what was becoming obvious was that you couldn't run a business with only one product. For the nonce, Olivier had four products in mind: rosemary shampoo, chamomile shampoo, juniper shampoo, cedar shampoo.

Only the first was already on sale. As for the others . . . to make them, you need the basic essences, which cost an arm and leg. They're available, that he knows, but he's not sure where. Somewhere in the Maritime Alps, he's told.

On the side of the road between Colle-sur-Loup and Bar-sur-Loup, an enormous building rose in earlier days, adorned with a towering brick smokestack erected either when the place was an army barracks or, later, a factory of some sort. Today, these words, black on a white background, adorn its façade:

MANE & SONS

Pure and simple. But the day when Olivier drove into the immense parking lot and parked his old 2CV in next to an impressive and, let's face it, arrogant lineup of other cars, he had the feeling that Mane & Sons belonged to some futuristic world of glass and precast concrete. It was an immense complex filled with twenty-liter demijohns of mysterious products. Each liter, he knew, was worth a small fortune. At night, over this paradise of scents, shone, in bright blue letters, the words that had made the family fortune:

MANE & SONS
AROMATIC PRODUCTS

Mane & Sons was a citadel, its secret methods of aromatic manufacture jealously guarded for perhaps a century. Mane & Sons was where dreams became reality. And Olivier arrived there — still penniless, but this time at least not dragging his trusty still behind.

I can picture him in the office of M. Mane himself, saying, "The fact is, I don't have any money, but I really want to make . . ."

At which point he took out his solitary bottle, devoid of any label and whose contents, given its endless peregrinations, were dubious at best, and plunked it down on the desk.

I can also picture the big boss himself, stupefied as he eyed this nameless bottle and stared at the twenty-three-year-old man standing in front of him, who by his own admission had no diploma, who naively admitted that he had no knowledge of chemistry, not to mention aromatic chemistry, but who wanted to make something, create something.

"What's your company's name?"

"L'Occitane."

"L'Occitane . . . l'Occitane."

Did the all-powerful CEO of the colossal enterprise perhaps hark back to the time, not all that long ago, when he was a little fish compared to the perfume giants of Grasse? I doubt it, for in fact the perfume giants and Mane & Sons grew and prospered together, not as David to Goliath. In any case, here he found himself, as if by instinct, using the familiar *tu* form of address with this neophyte.

Mane sized the young man up, evaluated him with

a single look, remembered his opening phrase: "I don't have any money, but I really want to make..."

M. Mane, CEO, was surely pressed for time. All sorts of urgent questions no doubt awaited beyond the closed door — telephone calls, telex messages, all demanding immediate answers. He got to his feet, pushed back his chair, proffered his hand to the supplicant, picked up a perfume bottle on the table, handed it to Olivier, then escorted the young man to the threshold of his office door.

"Okay, it's a deal," he said. "Ask me for whatever you need. I'm with you!" More than the 50,000-franc "gift" of trade secrets from Botte, this show of support from a perfume baron made all the difference. Not only was M. Mane not asking him for any down payment, he was also offering him extremely generous payment terms on the essential oils he was furnishing Olivier.

Olivier gave up his job as a lycée administrator, but not his analysis. He was living with a woman other than his wife, but that relationship wasn't working either. The only thing working was l'Occitane. The goal, and the path to that goal, was clearly l'Occitane.

> I distilled like crazy. I manufactured shampoos,
> I sold them in every boutique I could find,
> I filled bottle after bottle, pasted the labels
> on myself, and then loaded them in my 2CV
> and hit the road. I was helped by some of
> my former students from the lycée. And then

there were, more than anyone else, Jacky and Johnny. All Jacky wanted to do was earn a little money so he could take off for Latin America. Johnny was my neighbor. He saw me with my crazy still.

"What do you make with that?" he wanted to know.

"Aromatic products," I said.

"Really? You know what, I have a little truck. If you want, I can make some deliveries for you."

Nineteen seventy-six was drawing to a close, and I was working like crazy, but I was bringing in just enough to pay one employee. A salaried person! Which was more than I was getting. I did pay my psychoanalyst, which was becoming more and more expensive as the analysis went on. I hadn't the foggiest notion about accounting. I knew that so far I had lost 70,000 francs somewhere along the way. That was a paper loss, because the way things worked with the fledgling l'Occitane, someone did a job for you and you bought him lunch or dinner, or a vacation. You gave him what he asked for. When it came to money, I got everything backward. I couldn't keep track of what was coming in and going out. All I knew was that my products were selling. I couldn't keep up with demand. I'd kept my promise to

Mme. Clément, and she'd reordered half a dozen times, which told me the public liked what it was seeing; my products were in sync with the public's growing taste for natural products, combined with a growing awareness of things Provençal. So despite my total ignorance of administration, the business was working! In 1976 my business generated some 200,000 francs. By mid-year 1977, I'd already racked up 700,000 francs.

It should also be borne in mind — something l'Occitane's founder failed to take into account — that this enterprise took wing during a serious economic downturn brought on by the oil crisis of 1973, which proved that the products Olivier was making corresponded to something basic, like bread and water.

At roughly that same time there appeared in Manosque, at the corner of the rue Bon-Repos — "Sleep Well Street" — a secondary market not far from the chief market of that city, on the site where a building had been demolished and that had hurriedly been baptized Marcel Pagnol Square. The first people to take up their posts there were two or three farmers dedicated to organic farming — in other words, growing crops without chemical fertilizers or fungicides. Most of them were there for good reasons, having practiced conventional farming for years and seen the sad results: a number of their clients falling ill from the products used in their crops. Some, in fact, had died.

It was in the context of this new little revolutionary cell of farmers, among the crates of organically pure fruits and vegetables, that l'Occitane set up shop. It was an overnight sensation: people literally snatched its products off the stand. It was a classic case of word of mouth. From their market basket filled with natural produce, they'd take out the little bottle of l'Occitane shampoo or lotion, a bottle with no adornments, simplicity itself, and tout it to their friends and neighbors. This kernel of customers grew and grew — *snowballed* is doubtless the term — to such a degree that Olivier managed, between two sessions of psychoanalysis, to repair to Aux Deux Garçons in Aix-en-Provence, this time not as a waiter but as a paying customer. And there another miracle awaited him.

On the terrace of this world-famous café, to which everyone should pay at least one visit in his or her life, a stunning creature was often seen, sometimes bathed in golden sunlight, sometimes half hidden in the shadows of the linden trees. Around her gravitated as many would-be suitors as, in Ithaca in days of yore, besieged fair Penelope, Ulysses's wife.

Most of these young blades were veterans of the May 1968 "revolution." Either they had grown wiser with age, or they had put their youthful idealism behind them, for their only jousts in these days were those of love. Their world-shaking ideals had devolved into a single, often humiliating quest: to win a woman's heart. Most of them were Olivier's former school friends, the same ones who raised a hue and cry when this sleeping dreamer had evolved into a dreamer who was wide awake, who had pestered him with so many life questions that he had sought refuge in psychoanalysis. Today they had become lawyers and teachers and psychologists — in any event, completely integrated into, and in the employ of, society. They were well off, glib, keeping themselves physically in good shape, with clean hands and well-manicured nails. Some of them, sensing where the future lay, were already, in those early days, into computers.

Armed with a smattering of beauty-care elixirs in his knapsack, and that ineffable scent of l'Occitane with which he is forever imbued, Olivier — nondescript, colorless, shy, and retiring — was no match for all these birds of paradise dancing the nuptial pavane. As for his hands, he tried to hide them, for they were red and rough, a worker's hands. There's no way you can spend all day picking rosemary and tending a still without your hands paying the price.

Olivier was mesmerized by this apparition surrounded by so many suitors that they constitute a veritable boardroom of would-be lovers. Was this Marie-Paule — for that was the name of the flame around which the moths fluttered — a classic beauty? After so many years of seeing her evolve, I'm in no position to judge. Suffice it to say that she was — and is — extraordinary, in the true sense of the word. She was like no-body else on the face of the world. Incapable of such emulation, she made no effort to model herself on some current icon. Is that why she was indescribable — because there were no points of comparison?

She was strikingly graceful — a trifle tall, perhaps, but everything about her was harmonious. In a crowd she was the one you would single out. "Classy" was how most people would describe her, but that's too easy — countless other women have what is known as "class." She had neither the allure, nor the studied walk, of a model. She doubtless wore clothes of other colors, but I never saw her in anything but black, and that's the way I picture her today. Somehow she knew how to make black her own, either consciously or unconsciously.

But there's more: this atypical creature who, God knows how, attracted men as bees to honey, was pos-sessed of a voice at once unusual and deep, like the un-dertow of the sea, a voice that you encounter but once in your life, a voice so even in its intonation, it's impos-sible to differentiate whether it's expressing anger, joy, or despair. Seated there on his terrace chair, Olivier lis-tened to this voice that was half his own; until they met, he felt, both he and she were incomplete beings.

At that point Olivier, who had separated from his wife, was living with a female writer who, seeing him mesmerized by this creature Marie-Paule, said to him: "Don't even think about it! You'll never have her!"

Strange words, copied from the Book of Men,

spoken by a woman showing solidarity with other women. What does that mean, really, "have her"? Even to get close to her would be a kind of victory. For Olivier, to touch her, even brush up against her, would be seventh heaven.

He conjured, he dreamed up a dozen scenarios, he thought only of her day and night. Eschewing the idea of playing the dandy, of emulating his ex–colleagues with their fashionable suits, he went out and bought himself a corduroy suit (and I suspect he bought it secondhand, if he could).

"She was perfectly at ease in her bourgeois Aix milieu," Olivier remembers. "You see, it was tough to make any kind of impression on Marie–Paule. I was a nobody; she was a great beauty, the object of everyone's desire in Aix — all the young intellectuals, at least. All I could do to compete was go out and buy this ridiculous corduroy suit. What was more, I had a pair of good shoes, Clark's, but the laces had broken, so I'd tied them with pieces of string. To make matters even worse, the damn suit was far too big for me, so I looked totally ridiculous in it. But in the end that's what I think made Marie–Paule give in, because I was so wildly different, so far from what was considered the seductive norm for the handsome young blades of the era."

The period we'll call "Winning Marie–Paule" was a strange one in the life of Olivier Baussan. A philosophy professor introduced him to a certain M. Francesse, a

professor at the Collège de France, a man who epito-
mized elegance, an epicurean who had made the deci-
sion to turn his back on urban life and savor the
solitude and beauty of Provence. In any event, this so-
phisticated gentleman was intrigued by the enigma that
he saw in Olivier at this stage of his evolution. He
wanted to take this country bumpkin and introduce
him to the finer things of life, so he invited him to visit
his house near the town of Apt. Now, *house* is not a fair
term, for Francesse owned one of those magical properties that seems constructed for the sole purpose of making its inhabitants happy, long before the hordes of
people from all over the world descended upon the
Luberon simply to boast that they lived there. For
whatever reason, Francesse had offered Olivier free
reign of his property, to come and go as he pleased, to
feel completely at home there.

In addition to its cypress trees, its endless rose garden, its pergolas overwhelmed with wisteria, its cherry
trees planted not for their fruits but for the beauty of
their flowers in spring, this extraordinary property was
equipped with, among other things, an Olympic-sized
swimming pool.

One night in Aix, Olivier managed to work up the
courage to invite Marie-Paule to what he described to
her as a big bash over at Francesse's; there would, he said,
be lots of interesting people, and the champagne would
flow freely. He didn't mention the swimming pool. In
those days, in Aix-en-Provence, there weren't that many.

When Marie-Paule arrived in the tiny village of Buoux, where the professor lived, the only other person there was Olivier — plus the roses and wisteria, of course. It was a beautiful summer night, more than enough to turn that sumptuous setting into the first — and most memorable — moment of their life together. Doubtless on the edge of that romantic, oversize swimming pool, in the silence and darkness of that magical night, their destiny was sealed — Romeo and Juliet, souls joined forever.

How can I relate a life that suddenly takes wing and soars? Once he met Marie-Paule, Olivier dropped his psychoanalysis. He bid his past good-bye. From now on, there would be only l'Occitane and Marie-Paule. It should be noted to her credit that when Marie-Paule's mother first laid eyes on Olivier, all decked out in his oversize corduroy suit and Clark shoes with string for laces, she pulled her daughter aside and said to her, "If you want my advice, young lady, I'd grab that one before he gets away!"

Despite all the vicissitudes of lost loves, Olivier retained throughout the years an undying friendship with his mother-in-law. But for the moment she had no idea that l'Occitane would devour everyone! Marie-Paule; her mother; Johnny and Jacky, who both thought this would be a brief stint of no more than six months; all those who from the start threw themselves into l'Occitane, body and soul.

*   *   *

Marked by the sign of l'Occitane, there stood an open-air shed on the rue des Roses — "Roses Road" — in Manosque. (This city, which seems to be ashamed of its past, its originality, still bears street names that recall its ancient mystery: Lilac Street, Wisteria Dead End, Linden Tree Street, Roses Road.) And it was on the rue des Roses, suitably, that the child named l'Occitane began to grow up. Olivier commissioned his brother, an accomplished ironmonger, to build him a smaller, more efficient, portable still. And since Johnny's truck was close to giving up the ghost, Olivier had a brilliant idea: for 500 francs he bought the hearse owned by the village of Volx, a transaction good for both parties. On the one hand, Olivier now had an impressive, albeit weary, vehicle on which he could emblazon the name l'Occitane in gold letters on a black background. On the other hand, the village could now buy for itself the brand-new hearse it had long dreamed of, which in the coming years would be so greatly appreciated by the dead-in-waiting.

"In 1977," Olivier says, "the product line was still small and restricted: bubble baths, a smattering of shampoos, and a little toilet water. All of which could be made from essential oils without any need for chemistry of any kind. To expand the line, I'd have to have resorted to chemistry, which I couldn't, so this meant keeping to the basics. The products, however, were very concentrated, and what people liked about them was that they knew exactly what they were getting: rosemary, cedar, chamomile, and so forth."

L'Occitane left the rue des Roses because the rent had become too expensive; the cost of raw materials, advances made to clients, and ninety-day payment terms were squeezing the company's already fragile liquidity. Their new headquarters was a farm, virtually in ruins, near Montfuron, a suburb of Manosque. Here Marie-Paule, before becoming the enigmatic mastermind of l'Occitane, threw herself into the fray as a poorly paid, high-pressured worker. But let's not forget that Olivier himself was pressured and poorly paid, too. This was the heroic period when everyone involved gave his all for l'Occitane, without any thought of future reward. The farm they rented had electricity but no running water. They used rainwater to stick on the labels, and during dry spells they took jerricans over to Manosque and filled them up with town water.

The l'Occitane workforce now numbered four. Jacky, having returned from his foray to Latin America in search of utopia, would now settle for l'Occitane. There was also Marie-Paule, slightly confounded at finding herself transformed, virtually overnight, from a bright and shining, much-sought-after student into a lowly working girl. Marie-Paule's mother, a teacher, came over to lend a hand on Wednesdays, her day off. Her other job notwithstanding, she willingly pasted on labels like everyone else; not only Mme. Clément in Forcalquier but the Aillauds in Manosque and other stores in Volx, Corbières, Sainte-Tulle, Vinon, and points east and west were all clamoring for l'Occitane's wares. An intrepid adventurer who found the whole l'Occitane enterprise highly amusing, she was also happy to lend her school's mimeograph machine to print up the labels.

"So I printed the labels myself," Olivier says. "We used only recycled paper. The labels contained not only the name of the product itself — shampoos, essential oils, etc. — but also how to use it and the date of manufacture, taking my cue from the bottled water industry, which, I noted, always informed the public the date of the water they were drinking."

Let's stop for a moment for a reality check. L'Occitane sits ensconced in this blessed land between the Montfuron and Dame mills — rich names — in the midst of scenery so often described by the poets. Among these fields of wheat and corn, where nothing really happens, one can creatively educate one's nose, capturing their subtle multiple fragrances. These delicate smells don't always emanate from the flowers, but most often from the modest roots, close to the ground.

The wind blowing down from the Ventoux and Lure mountains carries these impalpable scents, caressing everyone in need or pain as it passes. Navigating through Provence in search of its subtle offerings — reserved for those who know how to find and appreciate them — would always be l'Occitane's mission.

"By 1977," Olivier says,

here is more or less the state of l'Occitane: the proud owner of an ancient hearse to make our deliveries; a farm with electricity but without running water; and a few pals plugging away to make ends meet. And then there was Jacky, who had to be paid. Fortunately, we also had Marie-Paule, as well as her mother. I manufactured the products but was no longer involved in the bottling or labeling: Jacky, Marie-Paule, and her mother took care of that end, the real linchpins of the business, keeping it together.

My forte, my expertise, was making sure the products were properly mixed. I knew just what proportion to add to make them come out right. I never had any formal training: I learned by doing, by trial and error, using my fingers, getting a feel for the raw material. If it was too liquid, I'd thicken it with a bit of salt; if too thick, add a few drops of water. I played with the ingredients, tweaked them till they came out right. Even when the company had grown to a pretty good size, fairly solidly on its feet, I continued for quite some time to be involved in manufacturing — at least until 1980. And as the weeks and months went by, the products did improve. It's like cooking: the more you do it, the better you are at it. But for years I also made deliveries, wrote out the invoices, answered the mail.

The key event, which really moved the enterprise up to a whole new level, was during the summer of 1977, when Marie-Paule and I met some people — the Froussards — who became close friends. Part of a group called Nature and Progress, they were organizing a show in Paris called Marjolaine, which featured all sorts of organic products. And one day Froussard said to me, "You should come to Paris." But to exhibit there costs money, more money than we could afford. Still, my friend, to whom I'm eternally grateful, for without him I would doubtless not have existed, said, "Listen, if the show doesn't work out for you, if it ends up costing you more than you take in, I'll help you out. I'll make up the difference!" How's that for a friend! True, he had a weekly salary — he worked for the Ministry of Labor — but still. . . . Both he and his wife were true-blue. To start with, they believed in l'Occitane. Our products fit in perfectly with their beliefs, their lifestyle. They drank only bottled water, ate only organically grown vegetables. And what did they use for shampoo? L'Occitane, of course! Perfectly in sync with us. So we made up our minds to try our luck in Paris.

Marjolaine! That bewitching name, with its fragile green logo: you want to protect it as you would a candle flame against the howling winds of the Mistral. (For those of you who don't know that blessed land of Provence, there is one — minor — drawback: every so often, unpredictably and unannounced, a cold wind, the Mistral, comes abruptly down the road — from as far away as Siberia, some people say — and chills you to the bone, even as it tries to knock you to the ground. As I say, a minor drawback.) Marjolaine! From its modest beginnings that year in Paris, it would snowball into a huge machine to take on and do battle with the mainstream marketing concepts intent on putting consumers in debt, seducing them to buy what they don't need or want with slogans such as "Buy Now, Pay Later." Marjolaine, raising the banner of those who hated the mass-market products they bought but thought they had no choice, mounted the barricades with revolutionary fervor. Modeling its battle cry on the "Marseillaise," whose opening line is "Come, children of this fair land, the day of glory has arrived!" Marjolaine trumpeted, "Come, children of this fair land, the day to say 'No' has finally arrived. Too long have you taken us for fools with your formula: 'It looks like food, it tastes like food, but food it clearly is not!'"

More than half a million people showed up for the fair, anxious to find out how to avoid buying and consuming adulterated food and doctored wine. Marjolaine was peaceful, passive customer resistance. No sound or fury, no table pounding, but within the confines of the vast hall where it was held, the odor and perfume of the country wafted, and with it came the whispered message: "To live and live well, you need quality, not quantity!"

Marjolaine was a moment when the world began to divide into two camps (and as I write, early in the new millennium, that split is greater than ever). In any case, from that crucial point on, there were those who poked fun at the "bios" and "organics," and others who paused and said, "Wait a minute ... *Is* there another way?"

Olivier again:

That was when l'Occitane really took off. Literally all the people we met at Marjolaine immediately became l'Occitane customers. That was also the time when consumer co-ops began to spring up. In cities large and small, a group of people would get together and set up shop, selling only organic products. Not only in France but Switzerland, too. All that went hand-in-hand with the growing awareness of ecology. In fact, Switzerland was the birthplace of the ecological movement. To be sure, this was a counterculture movement, swimming upstream, for in those days no more than five percent of the population was ecologically aware. But still ...

In any event, the crowds who filled the aisles of Marjolaine felt good simply to be there, to breathe the country air. It was the antithesis of the supermarkets, the "hypermarkets" of mass consumption, with their static-filled loudspeakers blaring, browbeating the customers into submission until they can't tell a cabbage from a cucumber.

At Marjolaine, just the opposite. The silence of the country made its entrance into Paris, so amazing that it created a hole, a kind of baroque antimatter. It was almost as if you could hear the birds singing, as those country folk — or those who aspired to be — wandered up and down the aisle. Tucked in among the fruits and vegetables stood the sign:

L'OCCITANE

And all those who were sick and tired with having their bathrooms filled with the artificial odors of mass soaps and artificial essences were confronted with jars of pure essences, exhorting them, "Do It Yourself."

"I was the only one there making essential oils," Olivier explained.

> I had these big jars because I hadn't had time
> to fill or label the bottles. So I brought up with
> me to Paris a slew of empty bottles, labels, and
> glue. The jars were equipped with little spig-
> ots, so people could come up and serve them-

selves from this source or that, and then we'd stick on the label and fill it in by hand. We had hit the jackpot. We were staying in a little two-bit hotel, and in the evening we'd sit on the floor and count the banknotes. It was wild. The following several days it was more of the same. It was crazy! I'd never sold as much in my life. When we came back down south, I immediately hired two more people. Our order books were chock-full. I increased our range of shampoos, making the new ones up as I went along, mixing new ingredients as fast as I could. The same with the toilet water. Two years later I had no fewer than fifty different products. At Marjolaine we'd stumbled on a jackpot formula: "Do It Yourself." People loved the idea of mixing and matching: we sold carloads of the stuff. What I would do was prepare one-liter bottles of a neutral base, a saponification base that I bought in large quantities, the old Texapont N40 that André Botte had told me about and that I have been buying in large blue jerricans ever since. Starting with that, you could mix up a whole gamut of bath oils and shampoos. It's the Texapont that makes the lather, and next to that I sold bottles of essential oils. I told my customers how to make the products themselves at home. They had the feeling they were

creating their own 100 percent natural products. On the label I'd explain to them: take
three drops of this and five drops of that, and
presto! you have a bath oil, a restorative, etc.

It was during the winter of 1977–78 that the first
store opened. The sign above the entrance read:

AU RELAIS DE L'OCCITANE
(THE OCCITANE RELAY STATION)

The storefront was painted bright pink and red,
like one of Corot's fields of poppies. It was on the rue
Soubeyran in Manosque, a narrow little thoroughfare,
with not even a hint of sunlight from January to De-
cember. No more than three hundred yards long, it
somehow managed to be completely asymmetrical
from one end to the other. Nothing was in alignment,
from its starting point, which was even darker than the
rest, to the far end: none of the houses was plumb, and
the adjacent lanes and alleys that bisected it were just
as asymmetrical. Still, it was a nostalgic street, just made
for a Sunday-afternoon stroll. Even today, the bourgeois who have run out of other places to stroll arm-in-
arm — wearing their Sunday-best shoes, whose heels
clicking on the pavement are the only afternoon
sounds — having walked from the Saunerie Gate along
the Grand Rue and the Hotel de Ville Square, finally
come to the Soubeyran gate. The clock, as intimate as

your living room clock on the mantel at home, tolls three o'clock, sounding more like the bleating of a Manosque goat than the sonorous ring of Big Ben.

Have you ever seen Manosque, and more especially the rue Soubeyran, on a Sunday afternoon? It's reminiscent of Dante's *Divine Comedy*: Abandon all hope, ye who enter here. But then, just as these Manosque women, bored out of their minds after the past three hours of aimless wandering, began to ask themselves what in the world they were going to do till dusk, all of a sudden a tiny ramshackle shop on their right drew their attention. Stumbling along the darkened cobblestone street, they reached it, on the corner of the rue de Poet, only twenty yards from the town gate — or where the town gate used to be, for now the street's a dead end. In any event, there, cowering in the shadows, sat the Relais de l'Occitane. The inducements to gather in front of the store window were legion. The storefront bottles were in such disarray that you almost felt obliged to go in and rearrange them, go home, and wash your hair. These phials and flasks, whose labels you could barely make out, looked more like magic elixirs than beauty products. Just looking at their contents, the wonderful ingredients they all contain, you could feel the wrinkles disappearing.

With some raffia, some sand from the nearby Durance River, a few well-placed dwarf palms to stand in for their taller brothers, a few nutmegs scattered about at the base of the palmettos like miniature coconuts fallen from tall palms, some cinnamon, and some dry bundles, and presto! You could easily think you had landed on some tropical island, some beach filled with shells. Even in these early days, the odor characteristic of l'Occitane somehow managed to make its way through the closed storefront window. People stood there, their noses glued to the window. They gazed in wonder at the antique illustration on the labels, which depicted a little girl wearing a laundress's apron, energetically brushing the hair of her little sister, who was seated on a wooden bucket. On the label was a water jug, a wooden stool, a bar of soap, and the words *pure vegetable.*

What a strange new phenomenon; how odd and yet universal was this little boutique that, like a morning in May, lit up a baleful Sunday afternoon in Manosque. Some of the little bottles were turned around, so that people could read the admonition to mind their economic *p*'s and *q*'s: "Don't throw this bottle away. It will be recycled."

The dawdling women retraced their steps back up the rue Soubeyran in a whole different mood, arriving home with a smile on their lips, the Sunday boredom gone as if chased by the Mistral. But on their way home, when they ran into their friends and acquaintances, who like themselves were killing time till Sunday afternoon was blessedly over, they stopped to gossip: "By the way, have you by chance been down the rue Soubeyran today? There's a new boutique at the far end. It's called l'Occitane. You should see what they're selling. Makes you dream! Makes you want to spend your life in the bathtub! And the fragrances. You should go there if for nothing else! It's all natural. Reminds me of my grandmother's. You know what I mean. The sheets all stacked in the armoire, with those little men fashioned out of stalks of lavender!"

Thus began what would become the basic ingredient of l'Occitane's success: word of mouth. In fact, it was word of mouth that turned the company from a tiny local enterprise into a worldwide success.

Around that l'Occitane boutique on the rue Soubeyran would gather all the modest people of the region, what they now call the "silent majority," who would visit the shop not just once but all the time, most often like-minded people who struck up friendships, who as often as not discovered to their surprise that their neighbors' taste and theirs are the same. Monique, the l'Occitane saleslady, was admirable at introducing her clients to one another. It's amazing the remarks you can exchange simply by passing a little bottle bearing a recycled label from hand to hand, a bottle you will shortly fill from the demijohn standing on a simple wood plank, which itself sits astride some hollow bricks. Suddenly the rue Soubeyran began to come alive with customers who had never set foot there before, had never ventured beyond the Grand Rue or the Hotel de Ville Square. Thanks to the little l'Occitane boutique, all sorts of newcomers began to visit the formerly lugubrious area, which almost overnight was completely rejuvenated. Even the uptight and the skeptical — there are indeed people who think that skepticism gives them a leg up in the world — even they, who thought that by venturing into the rue Soubeyran or visiting l'Occitane they were lowering their standards, who stepped down into the shop, for it is below street level, would enter with a bemused air, as if they were slumming.

"Good Lord! Good Lord!" they would say to themselves, "What in the world am I doing *here?*"

Monique turned these castaways, these shipwrecked folk, completely around in her own easygoing, no-nonsense way, with the absolute faith that was the daily bread of all those working for l'Occitane at this crucial time in its history. In its early days — and even later on — l'Occitane was a team whose hearts and minds were fixed on a single goal: to make it work, to make sure it became successful. Success had somehow always eluded most of the employees. Many could be described, in the words of the poet Jacques Prévert, as "those whose daily bread arrives more or less weekly." For many, it was the first time they had held a steady salary, had social security benefits, and had the privilege of griping about having to pay taxes. For better or worse, they ceased being loners and began frequenting the dance halls and cafés of the region, bearing with them the one-of-a-kind scent that emanates from handling the essence of rosemary, or of working on the original old still, which will always be the trademark of l'Occitane. Even the local drugstores and boutiques that carried l'Occitane products, which tend to be heterogeneous, ended up exuding exclusively the aroma of l'Occitane.

"In 1978," Olivier relates,

we moved to the little village of Volx. It was a brand-new villa, not handsome by any means, but not only large enough for us but with a separate bedroom for Jacky. We were working around the clock, trying to keep up with demand. Finally, I decided to buy an automatic labeling machine. But what I'd failed to notice was that the machine ran on 380 volts, and the villa was wired for 220! Filling up the bottles was no problem: I had rigged up some plastic jerricans with a faucet and a foot pump to inflate a pneumatic mattress hooked up to the jerricans, with the result that when you filled your jerricans, you created pressure. You opened the faucet, you stationed the bottle underneath, and the air pressure filled it, far faster than simple gravity would have. Fine. But as for the labeling, that system was really archaic. I'd bought a secondhand machine: you placed the bottle, and the machine applied first the glue, then the label. A super mechanical machine, a giant step forward. The only thing was, as I said, the machine was 380 volts, and our power source 220. To solve that little problem, I took an old bicycle, and I hooked up the gear shaft, the gizmo that turned the wheel, to the labeling machine, from which I had detached the air chamber. In place of the missing air chamber I substituted a training belt, which hooked into the rotating mechanism of the bicycle, which in turn was fastened to the floor. And on this stationary bicycle I sat Johnny, who was pedaling his heart out. And we were both laughing our hearts out. We were young. Life was a bowl of cherries: we were simply having fun.

One day, as Johnny was pedaling away on the old bicycle, Olivier jokingly suggested that Johnny turn his cap around; "Put your cap on backward," he said. "Now lean forward, over the handlebars, and you'll look like you're racing in the Tour de France!"

Just at that point a man slipped stealthily into the room unannounced — in any event we didn't hear him arrive, because the label machine was making a racket to wake up the dead. He was well-dressed, no ragged edges, the way a man in search of business, or on his way to a client, thinks he has to look. A proper businessman, in short. He was carrying a black briefcase bearing his initials. He had come to see the CEO of l'Occitane, Incorporated, and what he had found was the following spectacle: three young people splitting their sides with laughter at the foot of a labeling machine that dated back to sometime before the Christian era, whose electric motor, it was wildly apparent, served no purpose whatsoever. In fact, the motor was disturbingly silent. Whereas, hooked up to the ancient apparatus, one could contemplate a strangely clad racer atop an old Dutch-made bicycle, whose frame was far too tall for racing, a lad wearing his Ricard [a make of aperitif very popular in the south of France] cap on backward, racing toward some imaginary finish line. At the foot of this crazy stationary bicycle stood the company's CEO, in short sleeves, Olivier Baussan, and next to him Marie-Paule, completely engrossed in her robotic work, which was making sure each label received its proper share of glue.

And, one could not help notice, this ravishing creature was wearing a mouse gray worker's blouse, she who was always resplendent in her favorite color, black. Such was l'Occitane in 1977. But what that fledgling company was putting into its bottles and labeling was the quintessence of the lower Alps, the ineffable odor of l'Occitane, which would soon signal its presence everywhere in the region.

The new arrival, taken completely aback by what he had stumbled upon, took a deep breath for several seconds, the time to fall head over heels in love with the whole kit and caboodle: the labeling machine, the bicycle racer wearing shorts with his cap on backward, the ravishing young lady (despite her nondescript garb), and the short-sleeved CEO.

The gentleman in question was a banker. He'd heard people talking about this new company, which he was told was more than a trifle surrealist, so he had come to see what all the fuss was about. At that time, the old-line establishment, which naturally included the banks, had an innate distrust of the green wave of skeptics who refused to accept at face value the old, traditional truths. These "skeptics" were beginning to bother a lot of people a lot of the time.

At the same time, it seemed to reasonable people that this rising generation, this longhaired crowd, whose trousers looked as though they had been pieced together, who more often than not had never even finished school, whose equipment was old and obsolete, who had no financial backing and seemed proud of it, could enter the business world without somehow posing a threat to those already ensconced there. As Verlaine wrote,

The indignant sage harangues them,
The fool pities these dangerous madmen,
Children stick out their tongues at them
And the girls make fun of them.

Why had this banker come? Was he here to collect some delinquent overdraft? To place a loan? No one really knows to this day. In any case, he took Olivier in hand as though he was some backward or delinquent student. Olivier has his own special term — here not revealed — to describe this man, whose name was Cassemarec, and his stubborn insistence on teaching Olivier the abc's of business. He taught him the basics of what makes for a successful company, and warned him how easy it is to fail.

He urged Olivier to be meticulous in his accounting, especially with his deposits, and taught him chapter and verse of the commercial bible, which consists of a single sentence: "Deposit your receivables immediately, and delay to the last possible moment, by any means necessary, your payables."

"You have to understand," he told Olivier, "you have a product that sells, that people are clamoring for! Therefore you have the clout to negotiate excellent terms with your vendors. You — not they — should dictate the terms!"

"He educated me in business," Olivier says.

He taught me how to set our list prices. I had retail clients, wholesalers, some of the biggest supermarkets at Aix-en-Provence, St. Raphael, and so forth. But it was they who set the payment terms.

Our bills would come back marked, "Not Yet Due," which means they weren't prepared to honor them. So Cassemarec got on the phone to them, one by one, announced who he was, and told them in no uncertain terms — terms that Olivier never would have used — to pay their bills, which he told them were not only due but overdue. And God knows, we needed his help, for by now we had several salaries to meet each week, not only Jacky and Johnny but Marie-Paule and myself. Plus there were also all those government acronyms to satisfy: URSSAF (Social Security), CIRCO (Retirement Benefits), ASSEDIC (Unemployment Insurance), not to mention the value-added tax. As for that last-named, I had no money at the time, no ready cash, so I naively proposed using my receivables as collateral, showing them I had clients who owed me money, which as soon as received would be duly remitted to them. Of course they laughed in my face. So I wrote a letter to Raymond Barre, who was by then prime minister, laying out my situation. To my and everyone else's great surprise, he instructed the local authorities in

Manosque to grant me a stay of execution. That was of course an extraordinary exception, but the result was that the local government officials began to look at me with new respect. I've never tried to evade problems, always preferring to face them squarely. I also explained my case to the URSSAF, who had slapped me with a ten percent penalty, but after I wrote them they removed it.

I had been automatically overcharged, but they could change their mind! Then there were commissioners who examined our books. Thank God for our friendly banker, who taught me how to draw up budgets, who gave me lesson after lesson in business accounting. I'd go to see him at the bank in Manosque, and he'd keep me there for an hour, sometimes more, completely ignoring the other restless clients outside his office who were clamoring to see him. I raise my hat to this gentleman! Many thanks! He deeply believed in what we were doing, and therefore did everything in his power to help the cause. I tended to hang back! I was a dreamer, a handyman, a jack-of-all-trades. I hated administration. But he kept me in line, made me take the bit between my teeth, he focused my energy so that the company might show a bit of profit. . . . I was flying blind,

I have to admit: monies came in, monies went out, but what remained was . . . problematic.

That was back in 1977, '78. Also the beginning of 1979. The sleepy little village of Volx began to come alive as it realized something strange was going on: from our villa there emanated the fragrance of our endeavors, which one could smell from thirty feet away; in front of our garage was parked the com- mune's broken-down old hearse; and around our place an increasing number of shaggy, unkempt young men could be seen coming and going, people the townsfolk could never imagine getting a job, much less keeping it!

These "nature children" included a couple of ex-prison inmates, several hippies, and a number of dubious-looking young people of both sexes. But what is so incredible is that this tiny group of nonconformists were not only working their little tails off from morning till night, they were full of creative energy. Workaholics! Nine and ten hours a day was not unusual. There were even some — and may the good Lord forgive us all — seen load- ing up the hearse on Sunday morning!

Our employees had climbed to eight, then ten, plus at this point a combination secretary- accountant, who intrigued us all because she was so well dressed and proper!

The villa had become completely overcrowded, both for the employees and for the finished goods, which were piled from floor to ceiling. And the paperwork was out of control, as orders kept pouring in. Until now, Olivier's only relationship with the village of Volx had been that of a taxpayer. But now he was about to cross the threshold of the town hall and make a proposal he knew would bring down the wrath of the village fathers. "At Volx in those days," he recalls, "my reputation was pretty darn poor." But in that village, at the foot of the steep cliff, between Roche-Amère and Belle-Vue (literally, Bitter Rock and Lovely View), in the dead center of the fault into which flows the Largue, a trout stream that in summer is reduced to a succession of ponds and puddles between the outcrop of rocks, there exists a run-down old stone building that in earlier days had been used to treat limestone.

For as long as he could remember, Olivier had passed by the building with a wild dream in his head. From time to time he had ventured closer, making his way through the weeds and nettles to peer through the cracks in the worm-eaten door. The building reeked of emptiness, a place of vast rack and ruin. Olivier fell in love with the place; in his mind's eye, he saw no decay, only a site full of boxes and cases and machines. It was even possible, he foresaw, that the labeling machine might at long last be up and running electrically. Olivier's intention was to make a pitch to the mayor of Volx, a certain M. Domeizel, to lease the building. The mayor wouldn't necessarily be against the idea, Olivier surmised, but he also knew that the town council would be, if only on the grounds of public health. Translated, that meant that it did not want that building, which nobody ever even looked at, to become a lair for the dubious group of shaggy-haired young people, especially those two ex-jailbirds, or the bizarre Dutch bicycle affixed to the floor, not to mention that lovely young lady Marie-Paule, who was far too pretty to be respectable or virtuous. Besides, they suddenly remembered, it was the town's intention to turn this abandoned factory into an entertainment hall: that was the one point on which all the members of the town council always agreed come election time.

But even in those early days, Olivier wouldn't readily take no for an answer. He took his pitch to the regional chamber of commerce, to a man about his own age named Jean-Louis Bianco, who was in charge of economic development in the area. With his support guaranteed, Olivier went back and, with the mayor on his side as well, presented a concrete plan to the municipal council. His arguments were well laid out and convincing and finished with a resounding: "And what I promise you is that if we lease this building, I'll provide this town with fifty new jobs!"

The matter was next referred to the regional council, at that point under the firm hand of Gaston Defferre. A business plan was drawn up and submitted, with a request for a government subsidy, and quickly approved. The famous Old Limestone Factory, as it was dubbed, was duly inaugurated in the early 1980s. On its façade, in bold black letters against a white background, could be read L'OCCITANE. For the inauguration, the company even gussied up its employees, cutting their hair and washing their clothes, to reassure the members of the municipal council. And the following year, there were in fact fifty employees: Olivier had kept his word!

At long last, l'Occitane had a building worthy of its name — a telegenic building, on a site that would one day become legendary, for beneath it flowed the currents of the Largue, the stream where world-renowned local writer Jean Giono used to come when he was fifteen and play his flute beneath the weeping willows. The road leading up to the building was dangerously winding, with no fewer than three hairpin turns. On the flat area in front, as you emerge from the last of the hairpin turns, they anchored the original old still from which Olivier had extracted his first essence of rosemary. Today, it is still there.

From that point on, the long-haired, hippie aspect of the fledging company gradually gave way to a more normal routine, and on occasion one could even see a big commercial truck stationed in front of the building, it too bearing on its flanks the name L'OCCITANE.

"And yet," Olivier reminisces, "the fact is, till then I had still never made any soap. It wasn't till the late 1980s that soap finally came into the picture. Before that, it was all cosmetics — milks, creams, bubble baths, shampoos. . . . But in the back of my mind, I had always dreamed of making soap, because I had seen the steady decline of the Marseille soap manufacturers over the years. In 1900 there were three hundred soap factories in the region: in 1980 there were only three left."

With those thoughts in mind, or at least in the back of his mind, Olivier found himself obliged to go to Paris, where Marie-Paule's grandmother had just died. One day he happened to be in the Paris suburb of Pantin, walking his dog, a mastiff weighing in at a good 150 pounds (for dogs had by now reappeared in Olivier's life), when he stopped dead in front of a building that was visibly abandoned but symbolic, like his own building, of a whole other era, the 1930s, with its name emblazoned on the front:

RÉMY SOAP MANUFACTURER

Drawn by the word *soap*, Olivier walked into the building. A man on his way out asked what he was looking for, to which Olivier responded that he too was in the same business, that he had been manufacturing bubble bath for some time and had always wanted to manufacture soap as well. The other man told him that soap was dead, didn't exist anymore. He should know: his name was Rémy. His factory had been idle for years; in fact, he had sold his patent to the General Union of Soap Manufacturers. So it was that the two men, speaking of soap and soapmaking, wandered for hours among the machines that had been idled for all eternity, two soap poets whom fate had brought together. Olivier was young; he brought a breath of lyrical fresh air into the life of this elderly man, whose heart had been broken when the promise of production had turned into the rust of disuse. These machines had once earned so much money, and now they lay dormant, useless, their long arms dangling, without any raw material to transform into soap. Both men, the old man and the young, gave funeral orations on the demise of soap and why it should never have died. And when they looked at their watches, dusk falling, it was seven o'clock, at which point the old man said," Listen! I'd very much like to give this place to you, lock, stock, and barrel. I'll arrange for the shipment of all the material to you, and I'll come down and explain to you exactly how everything works!"

Olivier couldn't believe his ears, but he managed to blurt, "It's a deal. I'm going to make your soapworks live again!"

"The machines were pretty old," Olivier says,

> but believe it or not, one of them is still working today, at the start of the new millennium. And the soap mold of Rémy's father bore the inscription: "Extra-gentle soap." That same inscription still appears on every bar of l'Occitane soap.

That evening I called my close colleague Marie-Claire and in a state of great excitement said to her, "I've got great news! We're in the soap business!" I asked her to begin scouting immediately for a factory site.

Marie-Claire had been with us almost from the start. She had as it were seen the baby come into the world and had helped it learn to walk. When she arrived, there were no more than seven or eight employees to share the burden of trying to make some semblance of order out of the administrative chaos of the company, which was beginning to sap the energies of everyone involved. Starting as a part-time secretary-accountant, she quickly worked her way up the ladder, learning every facet of the burgeoning organization on the way. She was the model secretary every CEO anywhere in the world dreams of having. In fact, it is not too much to say that, whenever I had to be away, sometimes for weeks, she was the guardian of the temple.

Olivier came back to Volx and told the troops, the entire team, that at long last they were going to start making soap. Even as he was telling them the whole story of meeting old M. Rémy quite by chance, a phone call came, informing him that his generous benefactor had just died! But the man on the phone, a certain Jean-Louis Bénusse, quickly added, "I'm a very close friend of Rémy's, I'm an old soap manufacturer myself. We worked together for many years. I'm fully aware," he told me, "that Rémy had offered you all his machines. Things are a little more complicated now, obviously, because of his heirs, but I'm going to do everything in my power to see that my friend's final wishes are respected. I'm going to explain to the family that that is what he truly wanted."

And not only did he convince the family, but once the material was shipped down to Mane, he came and stayed a month, first to make sure his friend's wishes were carried out and also to demonstrate how everything worked. What was more, he refused to take a penny for his services!

At roughly that same time, there was another case worthy of mention, which demonstrates how fate often works. Someone Olivier knew, a young photographer by profession, Alain Gaulina, was sorely in need of money.

"Listen, Alain," Olivier told him, "why don't you spend the summer working here? As part of the deal, I'll organize an exhibit of your photographs."

So Alain came, ostensibly for three months, in the summer of 1980. And he's still here, twenty-plus years later!

"In any event, we set about making soap," Olivier went on,

and I must say our initial efforts were less than perfect. Soapmaking, it turned out, was not as easy as it seemed. I had invented a kind of tube to disgorge the raw soap pieces from their water. I have to admit it was a rather folkloric contraption, but nonetheless it worked, and the first l'Occitane soaps finally did appear. I had the brilliant idea of delivering the soaps in an oyster basket. I put twenty or so cakes of soap in a basket and added a few scraps of paper, with the l'Occitane label stapled to the basket. They sold like wildfire! Ever since, soap has outsold all our other products. And the mold we use is Rémy's old tried and true, which came down from his father and grandfather before him, so ours was the third generation of this extra-gentle soap. Later on I enlarged our repertory, I created various soaps as we went along, but the basis was always the same square 100-gram soap. That was our "soul," because those soaps were always made in the memory of Jacques Rémy, an homage to this forerunner who had understood when we met that we were kindred spirits. My enterprise, as a result of its becoming the trustee of the machines that Rémy had given me, became a kind of hereditary factory, and I was always proud to say that l'Occitane was in its own way, like Rémy's, a family business.

In short, as a result of this dilapidated material, of these turn-of-the-century (of the twentieth century, to be sure) machines, Olivier was going to transform completely the image of Marseille soap, which till then people had thought of — and rightly so — as this heavy, unwieldy two-and-a-half-pound cake. In the mid-twentieth century, women had other aspirations for their hands than to rip them to shreds trying to grasp a slippery parallelepiped that, among other problems, threatened to fall on your feet if you had the misfortune of losing your grip.

What was more, Marseille soap was associated in women's minds with doing the laundry, dishwashing, washing bed linen, and scrubbing the floor — nothing to do with the body. It was easier to promote l'Occitane's hundred-gram cake of extra-gentle soap, which was associated with ecology and dermatology. Little by little, people began going around saying, "You know, the best soap for your delicate skin is the l'Occitane Marseille brand." Alain, the photographer-turned-soap-man, made a bet with Olivier on who could turn out the most cakes a day; those two fanatics went head-to-head and managed to turn out 4,000 each in a single day! The major difference between l'Occitane's and other ordinary soaps was that these were tallow-based, whereas l'Occitane's was vegetable-based, and perfumed with essential oils.

"I managed to make some twenty different soaps," Olivier notes, each of which sold as well as the others. I've made millions and millions of cakes over the years, which was the real basis for l'Occitane's growing reputation. From a volume of 200,000 francs our first year in business, we grew to five million in 1980 when we moved into the Old Limestone Factory at Volx. It was phenomenal to move from five to ten million, and then from ten to twenty, and twenty to forty million at the end of the 1980s. In 1991 we had sales of seventy million francs. And most of that increase came from our soap products. They carried our images. I had asked a buddy to draw me a slightly naive image to use as our soap trademark, and what he came up with was an adaptation of an image long used on soaps in earlier days: it depicted a young girl with a wooden bucket, washing her brother's hair with a big bar of Marseille soap. It was an image you could find on any number of baskets filled with soap. Which meant simply that we had combined the traditional and current tastes of the day. What we did was eliminate the big cake of Marseille soap, and in its place show our 100–gram cake. But it was still the soap from Marseilles, only now in a manageable form.

Thus spoke Olivier of his great passion. One might think the time had come when he must take a break, maybe a prolonged vacation, or at least sit back and administrate this company whose success had not only surprised him but taken him completely aback.

Was he still groping in the depths of his pocket for his volume of Rimbaud? In any event, he would always carry it in his heart. The rest of his story, which is too long to relate here in great detail, would ultimately prove it.

Alas, by now l'Occitane had no fewer than seventy employees, and their average age was under thirty-five. I can still remember the sounds emanating from this joyful hive: never has any factory sent forth a more lively, more cheerful sound. They had all been taken either from the unemployment lines or from their own self-imposed idleness by a man who had never asked any of them for a curriculum vitae or a graphology analysis, much less an aptitude test. At l'Occitane, the work required of its employees was concocted out of whole cloth by Olivier for nonqualified people.

One must remember that in those days Europe in general was in the throes of a major recession, the unemployment rate was skyrocketing, and social unrest was increasing. At this time, too, the information era was being dragged into this world by forceps from the belly of a world in deep labor, leaving in its wake thousands upon thousands of unemployed, those who could not adapt, those who could not or would not leave their places of birth, those who were wed to the old ways of the world or to work that required only the effort of the cortex and not that of the entire brain — in short, all those who would never be able to adapt to the new wave of machines, to new methods, new vocabulary, or new ideas.

In stark contrast, l'Occitane was hiring people who simply happened to live in the area, people with few or no specific qualifications. They were virtually working at home. When it came to personnel, Olivier was always fond — and still is — of salvage operations, of throwing life preservers to those on the verge of drowning. How many of his former employees are on their own two feet today because Olivier made them stand up straight? For many, l'Occitane was not a factory where they manufactured soap and health products from essential oils, it was the kind of boat that the singer Georges Brassens celebrated in his famous song "Les Copains d'abord" ("Pals First and Foremost"), for the spirit on which the company was founded was still very much in force.

What was possible when the entire company consisted of ten or twelve people, however, was no longer feasible when the personnel roster had multiplied seven- or eightfold, men and women working in restricted quarters. So restricted, in fact, that they had to move parts of the operation to new sites: at Oraison, at Peyruis, and at Mane.

To be sure, the spirit that had motivated l'Occitane in its early stages was still present: mornings would always begin with hugs all around. When there were more orders than could be filled in a normal working day, nobody would gripe or balk; they would all bend to the effort till the job was done. And if that meant weekends, well, that was fine, too. But those who were working in the far-flung outposts, at Oraison, at Mane, at Peyruis, began to envy those stationed at the main office at the Old Limestone Factory, and vice-versa. Though the problems were not very serious or deeply rooted, conflicts did arise, and Olivier had to fly from one site to another like a fireman responding to a five-alarm fire. There was no question of delegating authority; he tried that, naming this or that person foreman, deputy director, personnel manager, in vain. They wanted to see the boss, and no one else! Any discussion with one of the underlings would inevitably end with the employee singing the same old refrain: "No, I want to talk to *Olivier!*"

Since everything came from him, of necessity it all came back to him. He had to talk endlessly with people who couldn't get along, intercede with warring factions, dispense justice as if he were Saint Louis himself, sometimes at the foot of the good old copper still, or standing next to a soap vat, or hard beside a recalcitrant labeling machine. It was more and more obvious by the day: all these sites had to be merged back into one. But the Old Limestone Factory, wedged in as it was between the road and the Bellevue cliff, could not be enlarged.

"The entire factory consisted of 4,500 square feet, all on the ground floor," Olivier remembers.

People were so tightly packed within its confines, they were literally bumping into one another. But on the other hand, that was the place they all liked and enjoyed. Everybody was happy there.

From l'Occitane's very first baby steps in the world until I was finally able to purchase the Old Limestone Factory, that site had been the object of my dreams. As I mentioned, when it was standing empty and falling into rack and ruin, I'd still stop whenever I passed by and make my way through the waist-high nettles to peer inside. And what I saw was a veritable Tower of Babel. For years people had covered its walls with graffiti, most of it unintelligible. And yet every time I went by, I had but one overriding desire, and that was to have this building! Everything I was evolving into, everything I wanted, I identified with this place. Everything I wanted to do — the trademark, the products, the essential oils, the tradition, everything — was crystallized in this place. I liked its shape, I liked the fact it was old, I liked its doors and windows: for me it represented the kind of factory they used to make, a place with character. I couldn't see any farther than that run-down building. I had no grand vision of what might happen if we outgrew it. For me, l'Occitane's dimensions stopped with those of the Old Limestone Factory. So when it became apparent we'd have to leave it behind, imagine how I felt. It was terrible!

But at this point l'Occitane was being pulled toward the future by its own sheer weight, and Olivier sensed that the time was fast approaching when he would no longer be able to control every facet of the business personally. Especially as the financial gurus were beginning to sniff at the heels of this astonishingly successful company, which, in the throes of one of the country's worst recessions, was showing consistent and impressive growth from year to year.

The first to succumb to these financial seductions was Jacky, he who had earlier dreamed of distant islands. Like several of the early employees, he owned shares in the company. Promoted to floor manager, he was now overseeing the work of others rather than doing the job himself, and, after all the years of hard work, he said to himself, Isn't it high time I profit a bit from all my hard work? One of the venture capitalists who had invested in L'Occitane one day sweet-talked him into selling him all his shares. Nor was Olivier spared the same fate.

Like all rapidly-growing companies, l'Occitane in the 1980s was in constant and growing need of fresh capital. As a result, Olivier, on more than one occasion, turned to banks and venture capitalists to invest, thus ensuring the continued viability of the enterprise. But the flip side of that coin was that over the years Olivier's share of ownership declined, until it was reduced to 51 percent. Given their investment, the avid bankers arrived en masse, armed with all sorts of plans and ideas to mine the company's obvious gold, and before long, the ship exploded, like a chrysalis in spring aching to turn into a butterfly.

While all these financial changes were taking place, Marie-Paule and Olivier were awakened one night by a concert of honking horns and screaming sirens outside their window.

"Wake up and get down here! The Old Limestone Factory's on fire!"

It was true. Vandals had broken into the place during the night. They had stolen the computers, defecated on the files, set fire to the cartons and crates awaiting shipment. The perpetrators were never found.

By morning, l'Occitane was nothing but a mountain of blackened rubble, of foaming bubble bath, which made any movement inside precariously slippery. The soap had melted and was a gluey mess, and the odor emanating from the place, once so pleasant, was that of burned and rotting animals that had been trapped by fire in their stable. The smell had drifted down to the Largue, which it proceeded to pollute. On all sides of the gutted factory the employees were huddled, sobbing and pulling their hair. Everything that only the day before had been elegant finished goods carefully stacked

The Baussan farm, situated between the villages of Peyrius and Ganagobie, was called "Pra de l'Intra," Provençal for "Opening onto the Fields."

Olivier Baussan, age three,
in 1955, at the farm.

Olivier and his older brother, Alain, 1959, at "Pra de l'Intra."

FACING PAGE: The Baussan family, walking through the hills of Provence between Manosque and Peyrius, 1961, Olivier leading the way. His baby sister, Pascal, is on the right.

The trusty, rusted old still, awash in a sea of lavender, 1976,
in full sunlight (above), at dusk (below).

Olivier (center), his brother Alain (left) and his mother Gisele,
1976, the "Year of the Still."

The same still, now a symbol of l'Occitane, stationed before
the Old Limestone Factory at Volx, 1980.

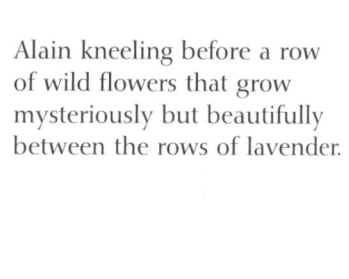

Alain kneeling before a row
of wild flowers that grow
mysteriously but beautifully
between the rows of lavender.

Olivier in Burkina Faso, testing the *karita*.

ABOVE: The first l'Occitane soap factory in Mane, early 1980s.

BELOW: The greatly enlarged l'Occitane factory in Manosque, 1987.

Olivier and two friends, at "Le Fare" ("The Summit")
in Pierrerue, Provence, 2000.

on shelves, ready to be packed and shipped the next day, was now black with soot. In fact, everything was covered with a thick layer of soot: the walls, the demijohns, the cardboard boxes, the crates that the firemen had flooded with their endless streams of water. There was no other choice: close down and move on.

For some time Olivier had had his eye on a building adjacent to the highway leading to Manosque, a building that the music company Harmonia Mundi, whose headquarters were in Saint-Michel and whose business was the manufacture and sale of records, had refused to moved into because they found it aesthetically not up to their high standards. A big building, 80,000 square feet, it had purportedly been a furniture warehouse that had gone bankrupt sometime in the distant past.

I can remember as if it were yesterday Olivier taking me and my friend Lulu Henry over to see the new place one evening. Olivier was completely depressed, doubtless wondering whether his company could long survive the devastating effects of the fire. As we approached, we could hear the menacing sounds of the nearby Durance River, which was rising to flood levels, while above our heads squadrons of crows cawed their lugubrious songs of bad days to come. And to top it off, the poplar trees were screeching in the wind like banshees.

The parallelepiped loomed before us, a strange, massive block, as enigmatic as a living creature, and like the factory we had left behind, black as soot, the color of a shipwreck after a fire.

It was a yawning chasm, a menacing void open to all the currents of the air, powerfully sonorous, constructed with beams of precast concrete. It was partitioned with cinder blocks hastily slapped together by a construction company who had mistakenly put in the low bid and had paid the price. They had been in such a hurry to finish the job, in fact, they had not even taken the trouble to plaster the blocks over, so most of the beams and partitions looked as though they were no more than a slapdash combination of gravel and black cement. How in the name of heaven was the elegant l'Occitane ever going to pour itself into this funereal mold?

Night was falling as we finished our rounds, and I believe that Olivier was shivering. He must have been turning over in his mind his 51 percent ownership and asking himself what, if anything, it was now worth, given the completely burned-out building on the one hand, and on the other the vast, ugly emptiness through which he was walking.

At this point, suspecting Olivier's precarious state of mind, Lulu and I raised our arms in jubilation and began racing through the building, shouting at the top of our lungs, cries of joy, as if we had just landed in Fort Knox. We wanted to make it known that we thought the future home of l'Occitane, far from being funereal, was a real find. Our echoing shouts — and there were many — were meant to congratulate Olivier on his extraordinary good luck. I think that Lulu even went so far as to ask him, "How in the world did you ever find this place?"

At the time, needless to say, neither Lulu nor I, much less Olivier himself, had the faintest notion that thanks to, and with the help of, this sinister warehouse, the founder of the company was going to make his fortune. But not immediately. In its present state, the building in the industrial zone of Manosque was completely unusable. A competent construction company was needed to whip it into shape. The only thing was, there was no time for all that: all right, you had suffered a shipwreck, but you had no choice but to go on. To interrupt the flow of business would have been fatal. Between the last package shipped the day before, before the fire, and the one due to be shipped today, there could be no hiatus. Fortunately, Olivier was still as adept at making this windfall of a factory function as he had been at tinkering with his ancient 2CV many years ago. His fixer-upper mentality was still alive and well. Before you knew it, the area around what was soon to become the company's headquarters was jam-packed with trucks and cranes installing those prefabricated metal partitions that, everywhere in the modern world, from city to desert, you can lease to make whatever configurations your heart desires, turning empty space into office or warehouse in a trice. Those who use them day in and day out don't even have to buy them; when you want a change, they'll be whisked away by the same people who brought them to you in the first place.

Into this labyrinthine emptiness, this metallic honeycomb, they jammed pell-mell the entire l'Occitane staff, compartment by compartment. Tense and irritable, the hundred or so employees reported to their new workstations, scarcely speaking to one another, wondering whether they were going to be paid that week, whether they ever would be paid, given the catastrophe the company had just suffered.

And while all that was going through their minds, all of a sudden the heavens opened, and it began to pour. In this country where it almost never rains, it came down in buckets. Then, to top it off, in this region where there is normally no winter, it turned icy cold. Picture yourself, then, working for eight hours in this metallic wilderness with the outside temperature a mere 20 degrees Fahrenheit — minus 5 degrees Celsius — manufacturing, packing, labeling, bottling, typewriting, operating a computer, keeping the account books, dealing with the incoming and outgoing mail, and so on.

People were constantly muddying the floor, for the compartment partitions did not always open into the neighboring section, as a result of which one often had to exit the building to move from one workstation to another. And the filth and mud outside would freeze at night, then thaw in the morning, so you saw people carrying freezing cold files, boxes, instruments, wrapping material, and bottles from one compartment to the other, and no matter how hard you tried to scrape the mud off your shoes, you inevitably dirtied the floor each time you ventured outside. So how in the world were you supposed to keep the package, or whatever you were transporting, clean and pristine? Thousands of times every day, in this anthill where fear reigned supreme, you could hear the same question asked over and over again: "So where do you want me to put this?" The trucks that arrived to pick up the outgoing shipments cared not a whit for these game but frozen employees, and often their spinning tires spattered the hustling worker bees with mud as they arrived and departed.

Where, oh where in all this, my dear Olivier, are your volumes of Rimbaud, your *Illuminations* and your *Drunken Boat?* Marie-Paule, still wearing her high heels and refusing to dress warmly for the occasion, steered her way like everyone else from one metal compartment to the other, which were like islands in the sea of mud. And, a mere 500 yards away, the rising waters of the Durance River bellowed sadly, reminding one and all that however bad things were at present, they could get worse.

It would be a winter of icy rain and snow, with temperatures dropping sharply, only to be followed by crafty, deceitful days of sudden warmth. This winter of discontent was also plagued by a flu epidemic that spared no one. But on the other side of this dismal coin, that period saw the phenomenal growth of the company. The number of people who were eating only organic food had grown exponentially, and they also wanted to bathe and shower organically, use only organically pure cosmetics and perfumes. So the customer base had doubled and trebled, and everyone was clamoring for l'Occitane's products, which were literally being scooped off the boutiques' shelves in droves. Yes, "boutiques," for the little shop on the rue Soubeyran had given birth to a number of children, and its already famous aromas had begun to attract clients in many other locations.

I remember one shop in particular, in a most unlikely spot. It was sometime during the early to middle 1980s, and the shop in question was managed by a trio of true believers: Hervé, Eric, and Manuella. I called the location unlikely because it was at the far end of the underground tunnel that linked the Lyons train station in Paris and the Paris Metro stations, just after you pass the honeycomb of checked luggage. Day in and day out, no fewer than half a million people passed through this lugubrious tunnel, looking grim and weary, lost in their thoughts, as if they were doing their best to believe they were alone in this endless corridor.

The shop of which I speak was located at the far end of this tunnel, slightly off to the side of the direct line of passage. If the term "entice" had not already existed, it would have to have been made up to describe this den, this lair that looked for all the world like a life raft.

Every product sold there came directly from the l'Occitane factory, and it carried the full line: the oyster basket of soaps, the aluminum bottles labeled "bubble bath," the adorable glass jars (which reminded me of those jars in which my grandmother used to soak her fat, late-harvest white grapes in brandy). Each had its own little spigot with which to fill individual bottles up to the neck, on which a sign was hung: "Do It Yourself." The modest aroma of l'Occitane wafted above the stale air of the Paris Metro and filtered its way in to them, as if to reassure them, invigorate and calm them. People who chanced to leave behind the somber tunnel and cross the threshold of the shop suddenly found themselves in a whole other world. Like Alice, they had passed through the mirror. They came there to bask in this other world, to cleanse themselves by contact. In short, it was as if they had passed through a purifying filter. They left the store with smiles on their faces, their tension gone as if by magic, clutching packages, big or small, to their hearts, for these contained their dream for the night to come. And as they left, they were followed by the comforting murmur of Manuella, whose warbling sounded for all the world like a bird of paradise. They clutched the packages as they would have a favorite pet they loved and wanted to protect. And to top the story off, the shop had the most improbable of names: Le Nez dans l'Herbe — "Nose in the Grass"!

Yet, despite its success, l'Occitane in the mid-1980s was having its own crisis. First of all, its customers, however faithful, were feeling the effects of the continuing recession. What was more, the expense of doing business was skyrocketing. Not a week went by that the company didn't receive some new tax or levy from the local, departmental, or federal government. Olivier is the first to admit that during those harsh recession years, he was worried whether the company could survive.

"The only miracle in the midst of all that doom and gloom was the birth of my daughter Laure in 1985," he notes. "She was the bright spot of the year. As for l'Occitane, it was the toughest year since it was founded."

And yet at l'Occitane things are so interconnected that just when things were looking their worst, a huge opportunity fell into Olivier and the company's lap. One day a certain Jean-Marie Colombon, the mayor of the neighboring town of Vaumeilh, dropped in to see Olivier and told him about an organization whose headquarters were at Chateau-Arnoux and whose mission was codevelopment with Africa. He fished from his pocket some strange-looking seeds, which he handed to Olivier.

"Do you know what these are?" he asked. "They're jatropha seeds."

("The jatropha" [*Jatropha curcas*; also called the physic nut], says Olivier, "is an oleaginous shrub that grows in the Cape Verde Islands, a volcanic archipelago in the Atlantic west of Senegal, which used to belong to Portugal and only recently gained its independence. The archipelago's roughly half a million people are dirt-poor, making their living mainly from lobster banks that proliferate there. And from jatropha. They send the seeds to Portugal, where they are used in the manufacture of soap.)

"Since you are soap manufacturers," Jean-Marie said, "it occurred to me that instead of shipping the seeds to Portugal, why don't you consider making the soap right there in Cape Verde? Think of the benefits it would bring the local population."

"He was planning a trip to the archipelago to study the possibilities," Olivier says,

> and invited me to come along. I'd never set foot in Africa. In fact, I'd never been out of Provence until I arrived in Cape Verde. Good Lord, what a shock that was. I went down to the local market and saw the soaps being sold there: they were imports from Portugal. But they weren't whole soaps, no, they were multi-colored bars — blue, yellow, green, all in the same bar. And I noted that in most of them were embedded strands of hair! What they had done was collect leftover soap from wher-ever they could find it — hotels, public toilets, schools — all of which they added to the raw

soap sent to them as an underdeveloped country, and from this bizarre agglomeration they'd make their own hand–me–down soap. I was scandalized, so much so that on the spot I turned to Jean–Marie Colombon and said, "It's a deal. Count me in!"

In collaboration with his friend Serge Lions, Olivier would spend the next two years setting up the jatropha soap factory in Cape Verde. The jatropha bush is a strange animal: the seed that supplies the oil can be used not only as the raw material for the soap but also as the fuel used to extract it from the plant. With the help of a big diesel motor imported from Germany, which ran on jatropha oil, they began making soap right there in Cape Verde. "I was so overwhelmed and delighted by what was happening so simply, without the slightest fanfare — using local products to make the place self–sufficient at least in this one area," says Olivier, "that I wrote a letter to Laure, who was just born, as well as to Laurent, who was fifteen, telling them that I had finally found my calling, that I truly had the impression that I was serving some useful purpose, which was doing something for others, not the way you give to charity as a means of lessening your own guilt. No, it was like bringing people fishing poles and teaching them how to fish."

And yet no sooner had he arrived back from Cape

Verde and gone to pay a visit to the Mane soap factory that Olivier — who thought he had just reached the pinnacle of his meaningful life — met someone (the seventh or eighth such seminal person) who would lead him into a whole new field.

This original soap factory, the direct descendant of old man Rémy, drew an untold number of visitors, curious to see these antediluvian machines making the soaps of the future. One day, among the crowd of tourists, Olivier met a Belgian journalist who asked him what he knew about the *karita* tree, which grows in a place called Burkina Faso. She showed him some photographs of this providential tree and said to him, "It's quite extraordinary. You should really look into it. The women from that region use its product, *karita* butter, as a cosmetic. I've never seen anything quite like it. I'm sure, if anyone could, you could do something with it. It's supposed to have magical properties."

"All well and good," Olivier replied, "but Burkina Faso is not exactly next door. But thanks for the suggestion."

Despite his response, he couldn't get the journalist's words out of his mind. Some time later, therefore, on his way back home from a trip to Cape Verde, he decided to make a detour and check it out. He took a small plane and wound up in Bobo-Dioulasso, where indeed he found precisely what the Belgian journalist had shown him: women selling little balls of *karita* in the marketplace. "That day," Olivier says,

I learned that that was how they got their pocket money. The product of their work in other areas, farming various crops, went to the family, whereas the *karita* provided them with the wherewithal to buy themselves jewelry, headdresses, clothing to make themselves pretty. In other words, it was their personal savings account.

The *karita* are gigantic trees that grow in the desert. They're also sacred trees. The masks of people who die are buried at the foot of a *karita* tree. A year later they are exhumed, which is what gives that special patina to African masks. So you soon discover that what you have is not just a simple tree but some-thing magical, a tree filled with mysterious connotations. So I immediately asked myself, What else can you use this *karita* for? I should ship some home and test it. Without further ado I negotiated on the spot the purchase of three vats of *karita* butter, each vat containing 200 liters. My negotiations, alas, were not with the local women but with some local traders, who seemed totally aboveboard and very pleasant to do business with. I also found a shipper and arranged with him to send the three vats back to the Mane factory, where I would experiment with the material. The *karita* I had bought struck me as top–of–the–line, very white, of a nice consistency, and it had a nice vegetable smell to it. I knew that women not only used it as makeup but also ate it. It was a fruit, with a nutty flavor. The outside shell is green, within which is an inner shell, brownish in color, and within that second shell is the nut that contains the oil.

When the vats arrived, we opened them, and what did we find but some rancid, foul-smelling, horridly gelatinous muck. The crafty merchants had stuffed the vats with some sort of residue, then covered it with a thin layer of *karita*. They must have figured they'd never see me again. In short, I'd been taken for a ride. But if they thought they'd seen the last of me, I had a little surprise in store for the rascals. Together with Alain Gualina, we went back to Africa. And this time — fate again? — what we found at Bobo-Dioulasso was a spanking new soap factory that looked as if it had never been used. In any case, it was standing empty now.

To make soap, you need coconut oil and palm oil. Burkina Faso was the only place you could find *karita*. For the palm and coconut oil you had to go down to Abidjan on the Ivory Coast. That soap factory at Babo-Dioulasso had been subsidized by an international consortium founded to give aid to underdeveloped countries. At first, the subsidies had included deliveries of coconut and palm oil, but apparently that source had dried up. The plan was to manufacture white soaps, of the kind used in Europe. No one had ever dreamed of making big cakes of Marseille soap!

So it was that Alain and Olivier turned themselves into merchants-of-all-trade as well as salesmen. They scoured the town, spurred the women into action, and awoke one of the village elders from his customary torpor with their resounding message: We can make soap here, and if we use *karita* it will be better than anything you've ever seen. Everyone got into the act, starting with the women's cooperative, but also including a fair number of children. The balls of *karita* began to pile up in front of the silent soap factory. A meager but useful supply of coconut oil appeared as if out of nowhere.

The natives looked on, amazed, at these two white men going about their business. They had seen many white men visiting from Europe and America, white men who participated in a banquet in their honor, who, the locals could see, looked at their watches every few minutes as if they couldn't wait to depart, or who at most agreed to take a quick look about town before rushing to the airport.

But these two white men were staying. They barely took time out to eat, as though food didn't interest them in the least. They were sweating. They had their sleeves rolled up. Apparently they were obsessed with a single idea: making soap! The local workers, wearing nothing but loincloths, bent anxiously over the mixing cauldrons, eager to know what was going to emerge from the mixture. Finally they managed to get a soap that, while a trifle soft, hardened enough to be exportable. And they made sure it wouldn't turn rancid.

"My original idea," Olivier explains,

> was to mix this product with the coconut–palm oil soap we were making at Manosque, and from that mixture bring out a new product. Given the self–interest of the women back in Burkina Faso, I knew we'd have no problem obtaining the raw material, the *karita*. And all of sudden the idea struck me: what a great handle! It was the women's money; everything they earn by gathering *karita* — and it would be many times what they had till now been selling at the local market — would now go directly into their pockets. *Karita*: women's gold! The journalists would eat it up!
>
> But there was something even more important that I learned later, namely that *karita* butter improves the skin. It's the best anti-wrinkle cream on the market, because it contains a natural astringent. You rub it on your

skin, and it regenerates the cells. African women in that region use it all the time, even into old age, and they are wrinkle-free!

Olivier and Alain made two more trips there, reorganizing the entire factory into an efficient and orderly assembly line. Back in Manosque, they began to manufacture and sell the first soaps to combine African and Provençal raw materials. At one point a delegation of women who supplied *karita* were invited to France, to Manosque, to celebrate the success of the new line, but none showed up. They were indeed the prime suppliers, but they were not allowed to travel to Europe, so instead they were represented by a village chief, clad in his colorful costume.

A grand banquet was prepared at l'Occitane. The local bigwigs, a whole host of journalists and most important, all the l'Occitane employees were invited. "The party was more for the employees than anyone else," Olivier says. "I wanted them to understand the full importance of our new line, instill in them the notion that what we were now doing was a major event in the company's career. Which it was: today the *karita* products are our most important line: shaving cream, facial creams, foot lotions, hand creams, *karita* milk body lotions. . . ."

With the presence of the African chief, the joyful atmosphere that pervaded this celebratory occasion, this new perfume of Africa that floated over the factory floor — which, by the way, by this time had been humanized, all the metal partitions long since banished — all the employees felt that night like explorers, lying in the shade of coconut trees. In their minds' eye they were whisked, on the fabulous branches of this providential tree, to Cape Verde or Burkina Faso. In truth, most of these stalwart employees would never lay eyes on a *karita* tree, but it had become a symbol of their work security, a little seed guaranteeing them employment for the rest of their lives.

As for the women of Burkina Faso, thanks to the new *karita* line, they and their families are far better off than they ever were before. And the *karita* tree itself couldn't care less. So long as it rains from time to time there in the tropics, so long as the fruit falls from its branches, it is there for the taking — unless the wind blows the fruit away. Some mysterious order of things forbade the fruit, and the seed, to remain at the foot of the tree, so that it would be carried deeper into the desert. Go and multiply! And through what countless mysteries does that defenseless seed, stripped of all power, imbed itself in this red African soil, take root, seek water in this endless desert, find nourishment from God knows what, to push forth in due course a frail shoot, enough so that it casts a shadow much like the arm of a sundial, and then, over time, grow as high as eighty feet from the ground, there prey to the torrid African wind?

That, in any case, is how the people back in the

Saint-Maurice section of Manosque imagine it as they hover over the vats where slowly the product of Africa and those of Provence, mingle and merge, to the odor of *karita* and rosemary.

Karité . . . karitas, karitatum et omnia karitas . . .

The strangest thing about the parallel ascent of l'Occitane and Olivier is how many elements, how many events, overlap with each other, to what degree good luck and misfortune intertwine, juxtapose, and conflict. Even as the Old Limestone Factory was burning to the ground, the idea was already germinating in Olivier's mind to spread the l'Occitane message throughout France, and perhaps throughout the rest of Europe, through the intermediary of a slow-moving barge.

The idea of that barge was born as far away from water as possible, namely on the Valensole Plateau, home to lavender and truffles, where the vastness of the countryside offers thirsty souls no more than the water shining like so many dead eyes at the bottom of the wells there. It's the prerogative of poets to dream of slow-moving waters while gazing at drifting clouds.

One day Olivier went to pay a visit to a Swiss friend, Andreas Muller, who lived and cultivated organic vegetables on this arid plateau. During the course of that visit, Andreas mentioned to Olivier the barge that he owned, which was anchored at the town of Agde. He used the barge, he explained, to hold meetings with other organic farmers. That discovery stuck with Olivier;

in fact, he couldn't dislodge it from that empty corner of his mind that was just waiting to be filled.

"At the point," he says, "I was looking around for some way to spread the word more widely about l'Occitane and its products, and it occurred to me that this barge was the perfect vehicle to serve that purpose. First, barges are slow-moving boats, which for me incarnates my notion that life should be leisurely, that 'slow but sure' is the key to fulfillment and enjoyment. Second, I was fascinated by the network of canals in France, in all of Europe in fact, for one could sail, if that's the proper term for a barge, from the south of France up to Paris, and as far as the Meuse River, the Rhine, and on to the Danube."

Olivier told his friend Muller about his overwhelming desire to own a barge, which he pictured meandering through the canals of France, a desire conceived in the blinding light of the arid Valensole Plateau. Muller set about helping Olivier make his dream come true. The problem was not finding a barge; these were a dime a dozen, he said. No, the real problem was finding a bargeman. These men were becoming an endangered species; they were being snapped up by other professions as the need for barges as a means of transportation was fast disappearing. However much these veterans in their blue peajackets loved what they did, however romantic their view of life on the water, the harsh fact was, they were now virtually impossible to find.

But as so often has been the case in Olivier's life, a serendipitous encounter awaited him in the form of an American woman, Hazel by name, who had decided to leave all the heavy baggage of civilization behind and, armed with a permit to man — or rather, woman — a barge, only lacked the barge itself. As we know, just such a barge was tied up in the town of Agde. So it was that she became part of Olivier's dream: she would be the captain of a barge called *L'Occitane*!

But hold on! We're not there yet. For the time being, what we have is a rusty old shell, the waterborne equivalent of the empty, dilapidated Old Limestone Factory in Manosque before it was fixed up. Love has its price, as one will see. Olivier Baussan is and always has been a perfectionist, and his next chance meeting would be with an enthusiastic ceramicist-poet, Alain Vagh. Wood and ceramics were his specialties. The barge was going to be cleaned up and made spiffy like one of those old pharmacies dating from before World War I — wood paneling and wainscoting everywhere, with stained-glass windows, jars and short-necked bottles. The entire barge, including the deck, would be covered with ceramic tiles. Vagh lived and worked in Salernes, the ceramic capital of southern France. Together they planned to gussy up, with all sorts of frills and baubles, this dancer they were bringing into the world. A slightly overweight dancer, to be sure — for the barge was on the chubby side, sitting low in the water and slow as Moses — but by the time they had finished, she would be full of nuances, contrasts, and colors nicely blended to harmonize with the poplar trees she passed, as well as the birch trees that lined the tow paths. Everyone who saw her pass, with handsome blond Hazel at the helm, could not refrain from becoming nostalgic, misty-eyed, as if a whole other era was going by, somewhere between La Fontaine and an accordionist from a few decades back, singing:

> On my barge tied up
> At the Saint-Cloud bridge,
> We may not be rich
> But we don't give a fig!

So here we are, with this former cement-making barge, once so heavily laden with coal and cement that its waterline barely showed, now setting forth with a new cargo, just as voluminous as ever, but this time of dried lavender, that are hard pressed to tip the scales at ten pounds per square foot. The smell of coal, dug painfully from the bowels of the earth by men who, like the horse in Zola's *Germinal*, raised their heads only when they heard the word *sun*, that smell one thought would only disappear when the barge itself was finally dead and gone, had now been humbly replaced by the brilliant smell, from distant Provence, of that plant of air and light, gathered by peasants whose skin was burned by the same sun those shadowy coal miners so longed to see.

In former times, this barge, awash with geraniums planted by the bargeman's wife and perhaps named, simply, *Louise* or *Marie* by the bargeman, as a token of his love, had now been rechristened *L'Occitane*. All spruced up and good as new, its role henceforth would be to diffuse its perfume along all the canals of the country. Its wake scented with the magic odors of Provence, it would bear with it the hearts of all those who yearned to cleanse themselves of everything ugly. As *L'Occitane* passed, as they watched this dream drift past, they could not believe their eyes.

This slow-moving vessel from deep within the country would spread the word about, and the perfume of, l'Occitane to the elite of France. Until now the people who counted (or thought they counted) had barely heard of this perfume merchant, unless as the object of a witticism. But Olivier's plan was to invite a judicious selection of opinion makers and local bigwigs to board his barge as it passed their towns and villages. Once they were on board, the barge would take them past their misty fields of dreams, the spanking new castles that, nonetheless, had been built in the seventeenth century, with their stagnant-water-filled moats, their summerhouses far too beautiful to be of any use, their ponds that still reflected back, though tenuously, the images of those lovers who, in times past, had leaned over to see themselves, their boxwoods trimmed low in the old French style of three centuries ago. And all that seen through the foreground of poplar trees on

the canal banks, soaring skyward, as if painted by Pis-
sarro.

Those lucky enough to have been invited onboard
would not soon forget the incredible luxury of the ren-
ovated barge itself as it drifted along the canals, or the
name l'Occitane. Past, present, future? The canals had
been so carefully and lovingly laid out that as you
wended your way through them, you lost all sense of
time.

Imagine, then, this barge emerging majestically
into the Seine, where for the first time it encounters its
colleagues, the still gritty working barges, which can't
believe their eyes, saying to one another: "Who in the
world is this affected lady, all tiled up and wearing perfume, as if she were some common hussy?" Still, greatly
intrigued, they would approach her as if to fondle this
lady ambassador from the south, who brought them
her perfume like a ray of hope.

Who had ever harbored the wild dream of opening a boutique on the ever so chic place de la Con-
corde? Quietly, and with little or no fanfare, this is
precisely the luxury Olivier offered l'Occitane. As they
moored their barge, he and Captain Hazel, who deftly
maneuvered her to shore, these two poets must have
felt a burst of pride at having accomplished what no
one had before: bringing the fragrances and flavors of
Provence directly to the capital of France. Having me-
andered along the canal of the south to the canal of the
center, from the Ourcq Canal to the lazy Yonne River,

the unique and now imposing fragrance of l'Occitane was for the first time about to stage its assault on the City of Lights. There it would unravel its bundle of flavors at the whim of the breezes of Provence, those gentle winds that nestle in the admirable poplar trees that line the canal banks, those trees that look for all the world as if they had been swept clean each day by some magic street cleaner. It was as if sometime soon, tomorrow perhaps, a team of Percheron horses, with lowered heads, would once again haul this heavy-laden drunken barge, filled with Provençal flavors, along the tow paths. From a distance, the barge seemed to be plowing the earth rather than breaking the narrow waves.

In Paris people came to visit the barge, tentatively at first, to dawdle and delay, then increasingly for pleasure, and later on because they loved it there, a harbor of friendship. Still, they couldn't quite get used to the truth that this whole idea had originated elsewhere than in Paris. But finally, since it did exist, they decided they might as well enjoy it!

A number of receptions were held onboard *L'Occitane*, a fair amount of business was transacted, and as always in such seductive places, people fell in love there. Before long the elite of Paris was flocking onboard to one reception or another. Doubtless the most impressive reception was the one held on September 3, 1992. The formal invitation read as follows:

Madame Edmonde Charles-Roux
Honorary President
of the l'Occitane Foundation

Monsieur Olivier Baussan
President & CEO of l'Occitane

Request the pleasure of your company
at a reception in honor of the joint venture
between this company
and the country of Burkina Faso
to introduce a traditional beauty product:
Karita.

With the presence of Jean-Louis Bianco
Minister of Transportation and Housing

Monsieur Serge-Theophile Balima
Ambassador of Burkina Faso to Paris
and
Madame Madeleine Kone
Burkina Faso Minister of Public Health

Madame Veronique Neiertz
State Secretary of the Ministry of Economy
and Finance, in Charge of Women's Rights

The barge will be anchored at Saint-Bernard Bridge
Paris, Fifth Arrondissement

The entire invitation is worth reproducing, both to demonstrate to what degree l'Occitane and Olivier had imposed themselves on Paris as well as to note that the invitation was designed and printed at Reillane in the Haute-Provence Alpes by none other than Yves Perrousseaux, the same man who sixteen years earlier had received the penniless young Olivier and agreed to print his labels! From the start, l'Occitane knew that what goes around comes around, as did, no doubt, the good M. Perrousseaux.

One other wholly different sort of invitation, to a reception two months later in Lyons, is again worth citing:

INVITATION

Olivier BAUSSAN & *Alain VAGH*
The Soap Poet *The Mad Ceramist*

Have the pleasure of inviting you to a reception
onboard L'Occitane
which for the occasion is anchored at
13 bis Rambaut Dock
Lyons 69002

Monday, November 9, 1992
From Five O'clock on

This reception is to celebrate the friendship
between Olivier and Alain

The Dream:
To communicate by sailing on this boat
which is ceramic from its deck to its hold

Further to celebrate rare encounters:
To Hazel, the barge's intrepid Captain
To Jean-Luc, a genius at taking boats through canal locks

There will be a concert
on the boat's yellow and green ceramic piano
Under the patronage of Madame Josette Samson-François

The invitation, illustrated with an original, extremely comic work by Ronald Searle entitled *The Barge and the Piano,* was sent to only 350 people, the capacity of the barge when it was packed to the gunnels.

Sad to report, the *L'Occitane* barge became a casualty when the bankers finally took over the company in 1992. Over the years, further investments in Olivier Baussan's love child l'Occitane had by 1992 reduced his ownership to 20 percent. That same year, the business group Natural bought up not only the shares then owned by the banks but a portion of Olivier's remaining shares as well. Over the next two years, Olivier still bore the title of managing director, but that title was largely honorary, and his decision-making powers greatly diminished.

"I had made the barge an ambulatory store," Olivier says,

a floating store, and it was that effort that led me to call *L'Occitane* "The Flavor Merchant," the way in bygone days people were called "Clothing Merchants" or "Rug Merchants." It was a barge filled with music! And the store itself was beautiful, a magnificent floating boutique, an old barge from the southern canal and completely, lovingly restored till it looked like new. We would take it up to Paris at harvest time; it was a communication vector. I was still attending the Marjolaine fair, and the barge arrived in time for the fair's opening. It still exists, by the way, and is still called *L'Occitane*. When I first came upon it, it was little more than a heap of scrap metal in a forgotten corner, but it was just crying out to be restored, to speak to this generation as it had spoken before to other people, other generations. By placing an emphasis on this nostalgic old barge, we associated the l'Occitane trademark with it. Through this floating vehicle, this waterborne barge, people immediately understood what l'Occitane was all about, why it existed, what it was aiming to represent. It summed up l'Occitane — easygoing, respect for everyone and everything — and when the barge arrived in Paris, it's true: it was an immediate success. People loved the idea that here we were, personally bringing our lavender harvest to Paris! Who else could ever do that? And barges are big! Not only could we hold receptions on it, we could also put people up if we needed to. . . . For me, the barge was as key an idea for the company as was my fixation about the Old Limestone Factory. Both of them were sleeping giants, old industrial tools just waiting to be brought back to life. It was if I gave them both a new heart and lungs.

It's hard to take when people tell you that ideas such as those are extravagances, unjustifiable expenses. In those days we had not had the foresight to document on the computer how many new clients, how much new business, that barge had brought us, not to mention the degree to which it spread our name abroad.

The financial people couldn't see it that way: "No, no! We'd love to buy the company but *not* the barge! The barge is your baby. Really, what a crazy idea, that barge!"

"I bought it back," Olivier says. "I deducted it from the company's purchase price, because it was absolutely imperative the captain's life be saved."

That's one of the oddities Baussan and I have in common: we love doing something that can change the course of someone's life. No doubt that tendency stems from our own lives, which were miraculously changed by what some people did in our behalf.

"Hazel was an absolute treasure," Olivier relates. "I couldn't bear the idea that she would be out of work simply because I was selling my majority interest in the company to people who believed that only the material is useful. And the barge remained my barge, largely for the captain. She's buying it back little by little. She's earning some money by taking in lodgers, by taking fellow Americans, who are delighted by their meandering nature, out on day trips along the canals. From time to time, when I have to invite some journalist, I often suggest he or she take a trip on the barge."

Olivier takes a deep breath. Even now, more than ten years after selling l'Occitane, he is still saddened by what he takes as the then new management's inability to understand not only the rich publicity and promotion aspects of the barge itself but also the very basis on which the company was founded and prospered. And it's true that, among his long-lost loves, the barge holds an important place.

But a man who considers action as poetry incarnate does not linger long over the fate of his past loves, even that of a barge. Olivier's life is like a ship's wake, where the turbulent waters churned up the ship's propellers soon revert to their former calm. The wake is the past, only worthy of being contemplated or assessed from the wreckage on one's deathbed.

Olivier's future holds the promise of many successes still to come. Remember that when l'Occitane was at the peak of its remarkable ascension, Oliver was still under forty. He had started the company from scratch, he had never strayed from what his conscience told him was the right path, he had never treated anyone harshly or unfairly; in short, he had never felt nor acted like a boss. And yet he's very wealthy. But Olivier by nature is not one to feel self-satisfied: he is always questioning what he does and never ceases to be creative. He always pushes himself as far and as hard as he can. Whenever he talks about the people who were with him at the start, many of whom he helped keep their heads above water, it is always with great tenderness. And fate has repaid Olivier in kind, sending his way a number of exceptional people: Alexandra David-Néel, when he was very young; Serge Fiorio, who is still among his closest friends; the Forcalquier poet Lulu Henry, who taught us that in the elegance of his poverty and free lifestyle lies true simplicity. It was Lulu Henry who, quietly and without fanfare, brought us all together. His house, always open to one and all, was the refuge of all our hopes and despair. It was through Lulu Henry that Olivier met the great photographer Henri Cartier-Bresson in the village of Revest-des-Brousses at the home of Dr. Levy, the grandson of Alfred Dreyfus, whose case of espionage rocked and divided France at the end of the nineteenth century.

In the same way that the idea for the l'Occitane barge came to Olivier somewhere on the arid stretches of the Valensole Plateau, so Olivier's interest in China was born on the tortuous slopes that overlook the Largue in Revest-des-Brousses, that same village where the Provençal poet Jean Giono used to come, at age twenty-three, leather-bound volume in hand, trying to sell a copy of the work of his youth to anyone who chanced his way.

There, on the side of the hill, the Levys — who had known more than their fair share of trouble in life — had a house that everyone dreams of owning, the centerpiece of which was a fountain that sent its waters rocketing skyward, only to fall gracefully into the basin below, a marvel of a fountain that would make each new arrival pause and gape in awe, one of those wonders that arid Provence reserves for those who take the time and make the effort to explore its depths. Olivier would remember for a long time this very special summer evening, this rare fountain at the Levys' house, this mysterious cannon of exploding water, whose base was steeped in shadow. And somewhere between two big leaves on the water a frog croaked discreetly, so as not to intrude upon the conversation.

In any event, leaning nonchalantly on the edge of the basin, his hand caressing the water, Cartier-Bresson was speaking of China. In his deep, well-modulated, self-assured voice, he seemed less to be talking about

China than speaking of a friend he had just left the day before. China was in his heart and mind, and he dangled her in front of Olivier's eyes like a diamond set in dreams, making her seem as close as the next hill.

Cartier-Bresson mentioned Robert Guillain, the author of the authoritative work *The Far East*. When he read this book, Olivier was hooked forever. At this point, l'Occitane was about to give Olivier a hundred times what he had given the company.

"You want the world? Here! Take it!"

And so it was that Olivier took off for Hong Kong, that city so crammed onto the slip of earth stretching out into the sea that it seemed it would sink under its own weight within whose confines so many people were crowded, it was like a storefront window filled with every conceivable kind of consumer goods; Hong Kong, shimmering like a badly flawed diamond in the eyes of all those who did not have enough to eat. It was through the furbelows and flounces of Hong Kong, this lush, extravagant, multilayered city, that Olivier would get his first glimpse of the vast country of China.

It was foggy in Hong Kong — it always is — so you could not see mainland China. One could sense it in the distance, feel its throbbing masses, a country held together by one belief, one tenant, a country so vast and so large, with its teeming population and plethora of languages, that one could barely conceive of its complexity, whose influence extended far beyond its borders. People always talk about the vastness of the oceans, but think of the terrestrial ocean that stretches from Shanghai on the Pacific to Brest on the Atlantic, those 9,300 miles of earth that separate one from another: are these two worlds, these two cultures, so dissimilar that they cannot be amalgamated?

Olivier took the plunge, not without considerable difficulty, for the red tape of visas and authorizations required to cross over from Hong Kong seemed endless. But finally he set foot in mainland China, and the first thing that struck his nostrils was a familiar odor, an odor buried in his distant memory. This memory went back a good fifty years, for half a century separates what the West has learned from what the Chinese are still laboriously working out from the original errors of the West, the way in the course of an earthquake some indispensable object is snatched from the rubble.

The smell that struck Oliver as soon as he arrived in China dated back, he realized, to Peyruis, to the big house of his childhood, without running water, whose kitchen stove was heated by coal. Here in China all these years later, the same smell of burning coal pervaded the whole country. There were still not enough dams, enough hydroelectric power plants, enough atomic energy plants, to furnish electricity for two billion souls. But, on the other hand, there were plenty of coal mines, the same bituminous coal that fifty years before heated the homes of the lower Alps. Like Proust's madeleine, the smell of burning coal made this native of the lower Alps feel immediately at home. Like benevolent dragons that reign over the households of all the poor, the coal-burning stoves in China are the equivalent of our own in the West; in China they're called *won*.

"I was . walking down the street, and I smelled something that reminded me of my childhood," Olivier remembers, "but at first I couldn't pin it down. So I stuck my head into a workman's house, and there it was: a coal-burning stove. And then a light went on: China today was Provence in the 1950s, not only the stove but a whole host of other associations: peasants who worked with their hands, not with machines; that same simplicity inside the homes, which had no running water. It was all there. I had the impression that I was reliving something: only the people and the colors were different."

Olivier was suddenly taken with the idea of communicating with these people who made time stop for him. Learning Chinese became his obsession. On nights when he was able to carve out the time, he loved nothing more than to focus on those square ideograms, full of mystery and elegance and profound science, which pose a major challenge for all those who don't have a gift for drawing. And when he wasn't painting Chinese characters, he was bent over the tape recorder, listening to the characters' spoken sounds. It didn't take him long to realize that what the Chinese took for granted, what they absorbed from birth quite naturally, these linguistic sights and sounds, could never be his. He was, in the modern parlance, genetically challenged as far as learning Chinese was concerned; he would always be marginal there. He wanted badly to share Chinese language and thought, but how could he ever do that if he couldn't speak the language, couldn't understand what people said? Still, he doggedly kept on. To be able to say "I love you" in Chinese struck him as absolutely essential.

"For three years I was completely obsessed with trying to learn Chinese," Olivier says,

> but during all that time what I didn't realize was that I was in the process of learning *Mandarin*. And that might well serve me to some extent to speak with the people in Peking but not with the peasants, not with the illiterate, not with all those who made up the major part of China's population. At one point I ventured into Beijing to try out my feeble Chinese, and after that I returned many times to China, but because of the language barrier, I was like a fly on the window, separated from reality by that transparent obstacle! Still, one thing I did learn, and learn well, was the importance of gestures in China, and how much they differ from ours in the West. Theirs are so agile; their fingers are so delicate, so subtle and slender! You have the feeling that, whatever the person's sex, you're always dealing

with feminine hands. Our Western gestures, on the contrary, are so heavy, so clumsy, so imprecise! To take one example, once when I was there I was invited to a factory that made incense, especially to see how they packaged their goods. Now, I know a little about packaging: not only have I done it myself, but I've watched others do it. . . . Presumably, I was invited there to show them how we packaged our goods in the West, not to change the way they did things, but simply so they would understand *how* we did it. And the point is, their packaging is so superior to ours, so deft and delicate, that I was totally impressed. And I must say that this was one time when my knowledge of Mandarin, however rudimentary, did help me to understand their processes by deconstructing their movements. For years I went faithfully to China twice a year, but then came Tiananmen, at which point the Chinese made us feel unwelcome and cut off all contact with the West.

It was during those twice-yearly visits to China that Olivier met, on at least one occasion, the photographer who is to the Far East what Cartier-Bresson is to the West. His name was Long Sin-san, and throughout his long life he recorded and documented China and the Chinese through his photographs. Old now, he has no more illusions and is a confirmed skeptic. The love that filled his soul for so many years has been replaced by an icy indifference. But what Olivier found in him was the universal presence of art, toward which, despite all his commercial trials and tribulations, he had always aspired. Whether in the form of the music festival at Aix-en-Provence, La Scala in Milano, the Fenice in Venice, or in the persons of true artists from Rimbaud to Serge Fiorio, art and artists have always been the ultimate goal of Olivier's never-ending search. Speaking of this Serge Fiorio, whose reticence is legendary, whose entire output of paintings has been gobbled up by people he loves and trusts, who in turn refuses to let "the others" see any of the work, Olivier nonetheless managed to bring together and publish the definitive book on Serge and his work, so that posterity can appreciate what this extraordinarily original painter has done.

Are we at a far remove from China? Not really, for it's the same harmonious impulse that has guided Olivier throughout his life, from Serge Fiorio to Long Sin-san, in a humble quest for the unsung or misunderstood. Praise is the last thing people unsure of the enduring value of their work, or rather sure it is at best passable, want to hear. Perhaps that was why Olivier, gently rebuffed by those who refused all recognition or admiration, turned toward the world of commerce, the world of urgent necessity, in other words compassion in its simplest form: shared passion, taking unto yourself the pains of others to try and help them through difficult times. This same impulse led him to China till it was closed, and would later lead him farther afield.

"After it was no longer possible to go to China," he says,

> I next went to India. My voyages essentially followed the same path as my career at l'Occitane. One day I found myself in the vicinity of the Taj Mahal, one of the most beautiful creations of the human mind. I had come there in the same way, years before, I had gone to Africa. This time my goal was to have the local artisans manufacture stone soap dishes, not only because they were both beautiful and useful but also because a share of the profits of each article was slated to go to Indian orphanages. As I had done with *karita* in Africa, here too I was trying to arrange for and establish commercial relationships that were equitable and respectful.
>
> In Africa I had set up an organization called the Balavoine Foundation, named after an African singer, now deceased, who spent his life raising money to drill water wells in Africa. When l'Occitane set up shop there, a portion of our profits were turned over to that foundation, to fund well-drilling in the Sahel region south of the Sahara. We also set up a

fund to protect endangered species. In other words, our products were a pretext for getting an idea across, to help various associations further their goals. This was more or less the time of the organization Doctors without Borders, a time when many people felt the need to help others. I've always tried to follow that line of thinking, and in my own case I understood that the best way to bring that about was through commercial exchanges. The proof is what we were able to do in a major way in Burkina Faso and to a lesser extent in India, and what I'm sure we would have done in China if not for Tiananmen. In fact, our example — reserving a share of our profits to further good works — had become so well known that UNIFEM, a branch of UNESCO, used our woman's cooperative in Burkina Faso as a model for what could be accomplished to the benefit of both parties. At various conferences and receptions, in Africa as well as more recently in New York, l'Occitane is invariably cited as the example, and we are often asked to discern the prizes awarded to others who have followed in our footsteps.

Also, our pioneering efforts in, for example, bringing *karita* and *karita* products to the world market have resulted in its being used not only in our own products but in many other enterprises as well, including food. And when years before I had been working with the local women down in Burkina Faso with my friend Serge Lions, I used to think to myself that while I was delighted that justice was being done, it was still belated, for Burkina Faso was a former French colony. In fact, French is still spoken there. So I felt that what we were doing was merely catching up, paying to some degree for the past, for which I felt personally responsible, for I knew that during the colonial period there were shameful abuses that needed to be forgiven.

It was in these words that Olivier spoke to me, as if he were all alone and speaking to himself, as we were winding up our collaborative effort.

Despite the spread of l'Occitane worldwide, we're still in the presence of the same Olivier who, at the Vale of the Birds, nourished his hippies, his cool cats, with rabbits caught at night in his snares. And if he still pumps his water from the local well, what better way to have a clear conscience and be at peace with oneself and others than to help a community stand on its own two feet thanks to the offerings of a miraculous tree?

But Olivier's fraternal impulses toward other countries, which multiply as the years go by, have as their necessary corollary not only the growth of l'Occitane but the fact that its horizons have now become so far-flung that no single man can hold it in his grasp.

"Even when I still owned the company," he relates, "I'd be gone for weeks on end, leaving a core group behind, the faithful few. But fortunately there was always Marie-Claire. Marie-Claire, who was the company relay brain, the person who, as soon as I had taken off for points north or south and was no longer immediately available, having absconded to Burkina Faso or China or India, automatically took charge."

But Olivier was upset and concerned by the increasingly onerous financial constraints, for which he was not responsible. He needed to delegate; he knew that he had to stop trying to supervise every detail of the company's day-to-day operations before it came crashing down. So he sold his majority share.

As noted, the financial gurus who bought him out were champing at the bit to make changes. "L'Occitane," they would say, "as great as it is, needs to move to a whole new level." Management consultants were called in, and the stockholders — who come and go — offered all sorts of suggestions that never came to pass. Innovative ideas were suggested to the people who swear by l'Occitane, but the problem here was that these are skeptical of any change. What the new owners of the company failed to take into account during the years 1992–94 was that the people who buy its products are a very special breed. Worldwide, they may number in the millions, but they are nonetheless extremely discriminating, people who have refused to submit to the general lowering of standards.

L'Occitane was the emblem of their stubborn resistance. To deviate, even for one universal second, from Olivier's charted path was anathema. By ignoring that categorical imperative, the people who had bought Olivier out were mindlessly digging their own grave. Waiting in the wings was a man named Reinold Geiger, who had long had his eye on l'Occitane. His initial effort to buy the company had been thwarted by the bankers who had bought it, but providentially, that gave Geiger time to see where they had gone wrong, the errors they had committed, which he would not repeat.

By the time he did buy the company, Geiger completely understood the basic verity that the people who bought his company's products were an extremely discerning bunch; that their number was growing exponentially had nothing to do with the basic equation. L'Occitane's customers are painfully aware of how limited our planet is, how fragile our biosphere, how important it is to husband our diminishing, and irreplaceable, resources. They are profoundly, acutely aware of the wondrous nature of Planet Earth, and they understand how important it is for every one of us to honor and protect it, to make sure we do nothing to sully or injure it in any way, so that future generations can breathe the pure air of Provence, as it circulates through the many creations of Olivier Baussan.

Reinold Geiger was perceptive enough to understand how important Olivier was, even out of power, to the future of the company. He wanted to retain the same tonality and the same tempo with which Olivier had founded and led the company through its early years. To that end, he made Olivier a creative consultant, in charge of l'Occitane's relations with the press and media, and also responsible for coming up with new ideas to advance the company's fortunes and image.

Nonetheless, when Olivier came to him with his latest idea, to add braille to the labels of all l'Occitane's products — Geger didn't quite understand how that would help the company's fortunes in the future.

Olivier's explanation forms what should be the basis for every electoral platform: sincerity.

"I explained my plan to Reinold," Olivier says,

> which wasn't easy, because when you come up with an idea that no one has ever had before, it's very complicated to persuade the other person that there's no direct line between the idea and its concrete results, that the repercussions are always oblique. To be sure, there are millions of blind people in the world, not to mention those who have such poor eyesight they are considered legally blind, all of whom would be delighted to realize not only that someone out there is taking them into account and recognizing their

needs but that, because of the braille labels, they just might become additional new customers for l'Occitane's products. But in adding braille to the labels you're also sending a clear message, in capital letters, to those who can see, namely that you care about and respect not just the majority but everyone.

In fact, this latest idea ended up being the most important of Olivier's entire career. For the notion of adding braille to the labels led to the creation, in the town of Lardiers, of a school for blind children, the purpose of which was to initiate them into the perfume industry — for what other vocation is so appropriate for the blind than that which requires an acute sense of smell? The school garnered the enthusiastic support of the English writer Peter Mayle, the writer who even more than our revered Jean Giono has, through his *A Year in Provence, Toujours Provence,* and the novel *Hotel Pastis,* disseminated the essence of Provence throughout the world. Mayle latched onto Olivier's ingenious plan and made it his own. It was through him that the American Foundation for the Blind contacted l'Occitane and awarded it a prize for its commitment to its constituency, and for being one of the rare companies to label its products in braille.

"It's not a question of recouping your investment," Olivier says; "it's candid, it's open, it's immediate. I can understand a CEO shooting down such a proposal, for it's extremely costly to add braille to millions of labels on every one of your products. Not many companies would support such a proposal. But the message is loud and clear, and the various associations for the blind worldwide were quick to communicate that good news to one another."

L'Occitane has other methods of making a lasting impression on its customers. Many years ago, the company gave as a present to its customers some cakes of bronze-colored soap in the shape of a heart. Every time I inhale the odor of one of these cakes when I'm bathing, I see my father shaving in front of a little mirror hanging from a nail placed just above the washbasin. He had bought the mirror for a song at some open market years before, and he couldn't do without it. Over the years the nail had fallen out of the wall several times, so the mirror was nothing but a series of jagged shards. When Father shaved, the mirror reflected a hundred images, which could not have made shaving easy. And as a child I used to watch him shave, and I marveled at how he could do it with that crazy mirror. Anyway, the point is, his shaving soap was also bronze colored, and shaped like a heart, and when all those years later I washed with its l'Occitane descendant, it was a truly Proustian moment.

L'Occitane is scattered along the hillsides of Provence, its lavender distilleries so many silhouettes in the blue slopes that mark the region, reigned over by silence, solitude, and wood smoke. The lower Alps are the national park of poverty, under which sign they should be protected. L'Occitane, which uses only these "products of poverty," is the emanation of this land. So long as these parsimonious lands of Provence continue to sublimate the modest perfume of its flowers, its herbs, its streams, l'Occitane will remain the vehicle of its promises and hopes.

As for Olivier himself, he leaves the company in good hands, like a nattily attired barge forever ready to weigh anchor and head off toward new adventures, new loves.